Previous Books by Jeffrey A. Kottler

Beyond Blame: A New Way of Resolving Conflicts in Relationships (1994)

The Heart of Healing: Relationships in Therapy (1994, with Thomas Sexton and Susan Whiston)

Classrooms Under the Influence: Counteracting Problems of Addiction (1994, with Richard Powell and Stan Zehm)

The Emerging Professional Counselor: From Dreams to Realities (1994, with Richard Hazler)

On Being a Therapist (1993, rev. ed.)

Teacher as Counselor (1993, with Ellen Kottler)

Advanced Group Leadership (1993)

On Being a Teacher (1993, with Stan Zehm)

Compassionate Therapy: Working with Difficult Clients (1992)

Introduction to Therapeutic Counseling (1992, 2nd ed., with Robert Brown)

The Compleat Therapist (1991)

Private Moments, Secret Selves: Enriching Our Time Alone (1990)

The Imperfect Therapist: Learning from Failure in Therapeutic Practice (1989, with Diane Blau)

Ethical and Legal Issues in Counseling and Psychotherapy: A Comprehensive Guide (1985, 2nd ed., with William Van Hoose)

Pragmatic Group Leadership (1983)

Mouthing Off: A Study of Oral Behavior, Its Causes and Treatments (1981)

Growing a Therapist

Jeffrey A. Kottler

Growing a Therapist

Jossey-Bass Publishers
San Francisco

Substantial discounts on bulk quantities of Jossey-Bass books are available to corporations, professional associations, and other organizations. For details and discount information, contact the special sales department at Jossey-Bass Inc., Publishers. (415) 433–1740; Fax (800) 605–2665.

For sales outside the United States, please contact your local Paramount Publishing International Office.

 Manufactured in the United States of America on Lyons Falls Pathfinder Tradebook. This paper is acid-free and 100 percent totally chlorine-free.

Library of Congress Cataloging-in-Publication Data

Kottler, Jeffrey A.
    Growing a therapist / Jeffrey A. Kottler.
      p. cm.—(The Jossey-Bass social and behavioral science series)
    ISBN 0–7879–0049–4
      1. Kottler, Jeffrey A. 2. Psychotherapists—United States—
Biography. 3. Psychotherapy. I. Title. II. Series.
RC438.6.K68A3 1995
   616.89'14'092—dc20   94–32447
   [B]   CIP

FIRST EDITION
HB Printing   10 9 8 7 6 5 4 3 2 1   Code 9506

The Jossey-Bass
Social and Behavioral Science Series

Contents

· ·

Acknowledgments

. . . .

Because of the very personal nature of this book and the vulnerability inherent in revealing myself so completely, I required an extraordinary amount of support during the difficult, often painful process of writing it. I gratefully acknowledge the editorial and therapeutic assistance of my Jossey-Bass editor, Alan Rinzler, and my wife, Ellen Kottler.

Growing a Therapist

Part I

Lost Child

1

Never Enough to Good Enough

This is the story of a person, a man who happens to be a therapist and teacher, who has been plagued by demons and doubts most of his life. It is about his struggle to overcome his fears, inadequacies, and insecurities, and how in so doing, he has been able along the way to help others who have wrestled with these same issues. It is my own story.

Growing a Therapist reveals my journey toward self-healing. It is about how and why I became a therapist and then a teacher of others who are following a similar path. This process of healing myself has been and continues to be the basis for what I do to help others. It is not that all my training and all the books I have read, workshops and seminars I have attended, and supervision I have received were not useful. They have been instrumental in shaping the way I function as a professional. However, the essence of what I know, what I have written about and taught to others, comes not only from these formal learning experiences but also from surviving, even flourishing, after a childhood in which I felt so downtrodden that I never gave myself a chance to succeed in life. Neither did anyone else. So, although this is the story of a life loaded with doubts, failures, and illusions, it is also filled with hope. I have been able to overcome many obstacles, both personal and professional, as well as to harness my pain in such a way that it has proven to be among my most cherished gifts.

Being Ordinary

I am of average height, weight, and build. While not preci$ some or brilliant, I am neither ugly nor dumb. I've never been really good at much, but I read a lot and try hard to prove I am really not as ordinary as I feel.

I had a hard time in school—not being (or feeling) particularly smart or popular. My grades were marginal. I didn't excel in sports, clubs, academics, or citizenship. I was conditionally admitted to college and muddled my way through the first years—mainly to avoid the draft, a job, and the real world.

Somewhere, somehow, something clicked. I hated being ordinary, yet I didn't have any real talent to excel in any area. I wanted to be smart, but I didn't know how. I started watching smart people—the ones who walked around campus with calculators, briefcases, and armloads of books. I asked myself again and again how they were different from me.

After giving the matter considerable thought, I decided that what distinguished smart people was that they read books, lots of books. And indeed, the more books I read, the smarter I appeared to others. Even by association, books had this effect—just the fact that I was surrounded by books, carrying them with me wherever I went, made me seem smart. People started to treat me differently before I ever entertained the dream that not only seeming but being smart might be possible. Here was a guy who barely graduated high school, who could only get into college on probation, who was such a mediocre student and test-taker that every class was a struggle (except for psychology and English), and now his teachers and friends acted as if he knew stuff.

And so began my quest to escape ordinariness. I read biographies of famous people whom I admired. I read the novels that smart people were supposed to know. I set out to make myself into a person who not only wanted to help people but who truly had something to offer, even if it was what other people wrote. The last sentence foreshadows my struggle as a writer in subsequent years. Once I had mastered what everyone else had to say on a subject, what could I ever offer that was new and original? Perhaps I was destined to be a synthesizer and simplifier of others' thinking. Although I aspired for something more, I decided there was no shame in that task. After all, at least I would be smart.

Throughout my early adulthood, I really began to move along. I started believing I was intelligent, attractive, creative, and talented, and so I acted that way. I had completed a doctorate and published my first book by the time I was twenty-five. Students, clients, readers, colleagues expressed admiration for my precocious accomplishments. And yet I knew that the only thing that disguised my complete and utter mediocrity was my desperate desire to distinguish myself.

My ordinary life has been marked by one exceptional theme which has permitted me the luxury of finding adventure: an unflinching willingness to take risks. Boredom, repetition, routines make me crazy. I pace. Feel irritable. Read more books. Go exercise. Buy something. Take up the flute. Create a crisis. Taking risks has been easy for me because I always felt I had little to lose. Movement in *any* direction has to be better than standing still. When I do the same thing for very long, I feel as if I am dying inside. After all, I'm so ordinary; any minute, people will catch on to my insignificance.

Perhaps, then, you can appreciate the risks that I am taking in opening myself up to you.

The Nightmare

My worst nightmare is that I would try my absolute hardest to do something, and it still would not be sufficient to get what I want. I would work tirelessly and compulsively, forgo sleep and idle play. Yet no matter how much energy I would invest, how much commitment I would make, how hard I would push myself to explore territory in which others have feared to tread, it would never be enough for me to feel redeemed. I have tried to make myself into the best teacher I possibly can, and if reviews are any indication, I have succeeded reasonably well. Each week brings a letter or two from some faraway reader testifying how I have changed his or her life. My willingness to be vulnerable, to expose myself, to speak aloud what others think but will not say, seems to offer comfort to others who feel as imperfect as I do.

As carefully and meticulously as I might research my subjects, document ideas, synthesize the contributions of others before me, and draw practical inferences for applications to life and work, it is my stories that people remember best and use to full advantage. On numerous occasions, I have spent two complete days teaching a hundred therapists advanced strategies for working with difficult clients, and what they recall most gratefully when all is said and done is my admission that much of the time I don't really know what I am doing. After this disclosure, the collective sigh across the room is so profound it resembles one big balloon slowly deflating.

My evaluations from students most often report how supported and validated they felt because I took such pains to present myself as flawed and human, to show that even with so much experience, I still have not lost the wonder, the doubt, the innocence, the feelings of impotence that accompany the role of professional helper. I do not pretend to know what I do not, nor do I act as if I do everything right. Likewise, readers of my books and articles may remember a few helpful hints or a particularly compelling case analysis or synthesis of ideas, but most of all, they are moved by my disclosures of vulnerability.

When I proposed to my editor that I begin a new book, one that would look at the inner world of being a therapist, integrate the literature on the subject, and investigate the experiences of my peers, he remarked that since it is my own open and transparent inner world that people most respond to, why not skip the other stuff and talk about the stories of my own journey toward self-healing.

It was with trepidation and a certain amount of anguish that I agreed to complete this task. As you will learn, if you don't know already, I care altogether too much about what others think of me, and I am most vulnerable when I place myself in a position of allowing others to judge me. Exposing myself as completely as I do in the stories that follow is part of my worst nightmare, since I am setting myself up for possible rejection, ridicule, or contempt.

Despite these tremendous risks in opening myself up to intense scrutiny, I have always felt that if this openness is what I expect from my students, supervisees, and clients I must lead the way. I must be willing to expose myself in such a way that I reveal my doubts and uncertainties as well as what I believe I know and understand. I must put myself in a position to be judged by *you*, the reader, even though you may think less of me because of my blemishes and flaws, laugh at my human frailties, or criticize me harshly. Since I am showing the parts of me that I am least comfortable with, least accepting of, least proud of, I am even more vulnerable to your quite legitimate negative scrutiny.

Yet I am hopeful that you will suspend your judgment as you read the disclosures that follow, just as you would wish me to do if our roles were reversed. Listen with an open heart and mind. As I invite you to enter my inner world, invite yourself to do the same with your own experiences that never come up to your expectations. It is from such study of "never enough" that it is ultimately possible to feel "good enough." Trust me.

2

Hiking the Narrows

A narrows is a geological creation in which erosion and drainage have chiselled a slim passageway in rock walls through which a river runs. The walls may reach so high into the sky, thousands of feet in places, that all light is blocked out. Often, lush ferns and rivulets of water dribble down the sides of the gorge. Waterfalls cascade through openings in the cliffs, feeding the river in its determination to reach freedom somewhere beyond. Always, there is the sound of water, bubbling, flowing, at times crashing through the ravine, squeezing between walls, pushing silt and logs, even rearranging boulders along its route.

Among the most beautiful narrows in the world are those in Zion Canyon. Beginning as a trickle on a ranch in Utah high country, the Virgin River collects contributions from the surrounding plateau, descending steeply through a fifteen-mile chasm in sheer sandstone walls. Shaded in streaks of silver, black, grey, red, and orange, sometimes polished to a blinding gleam, these walls are a masterpiece of the river's patient work over millions of years.

Nobody forced me to hike these narrows; I did so of reasonably sound mind and fit body. Yet this is the natural world at its most fierce and unpredictable. Flash floods can rage through the canyon with little notice, surging above any level where survival is possible. Full-length trees and boulders the size of a garage come crashing through in these floods, destroying anyone or anything so foolish as to tempt fate. Yet this is among the most beautiful spots on Earth, a place so inaccessible there is only a single entrance and a single exit. Once committed to the only path, you have no way out for twelve hours, trudging along the river bed, climbing over boulders that block the way, swimming through deep pools, crawling along muddy banks, balancing to stay upright on the slippery rocks.

Hiking the narrows is life at its most exciting, and most grueling. Unless you are willing to venture into the canyon, you cannot gather this particular kind of utter solitude, exhilaration, and exhaustion. Tourists at the lower end of the canyon dabble with the experience. Some take off their shoes and stick their feet in the water; the more adventurous wade upriver a few miles and then turn back, daunted by the never-ending turns in the stream, the forbidding walls that close in, the lack of high ground. Boulders are strewn everywhere, slippery with algae, wrenching knees and ankles, working in concert with the rapids to trip the unwary.

Even on my first trip into the canyon, I find the feelings of wariness and apprehension familiar. Every time I find myself in a predicament with no easy escape, a first expedition into the unknown, I ask myself why I am doing this. Now, as I hike the narrows, my back aches, my legs tremble, my knees feel like they are giving way. Water from a torrential thunderstorm drenches my top half while the freezing river numbs the bottom. This is exactly the kind of weather I had been warned about—at any moment I might hear the crashing thunder of impending doom. Nervously, I scan the sides for some handhold, foolishly believing I might hang on to the wall and not be torn away by the flood. I drudge onward, staring at my watch, calculating whether I might escape before dark, for once the light goes I will be frozen to the spot, unable to venture further without light to guide me. At any moment, I can end up on my rear, tripped up by a treacherous current. At times, I struggle in a whirlpool to get across a wide expanse or have to climb up a cliff face, over a ridge covered in slippery mud. There is nothing to hang on to; a single misstep and I will crash on the rocks below.

At other times, the way looks insurmountable, yet I know many others have passed before me. There *must* be a way out of here.

I forget to look up, to watch the walls, to enjoy the spectacular scenery. So focused am I on getting out of this place, I forget to stop and listen to the sounds. I am so hungry and cold and wet and tired that I don't remember why I'm here in the first place. I feel like a lost child. Whimpers well up in my chest. I swallow them and drudge onward. This is where I wanted to be, and now I want to be somewhere else—in a hot shower, eating Mexican food, asleep in bed.

Then all of a sudden, at a time I least expected, there are other people walking upstream from the lower end, my first companions of the day. I thought I'd feel joy and relief at the prospect of an end in sight, but I feel nothing but resentment. How dare you people invade my narrows! I earned this experience every step of the way, while you sightseers are here just for a quick glimpse and a photograph so you can prove you were here.

I am astonished by the vehemence of my disdain. After all, thousands of people walk this route each year; I am only the first of the day to make it through, and that only because I raced at lurching speed, driven by apprehension and foreboding that, this time, my life I would be overtaken by a flash flood.

Indeed, it seems to me that these narrows are a perfect metaphor for the parts of life that haunt me the most. I feel that my life has been similar to this hike, at least during those times when I was moving from one place or state of mind to another. All the ghosts who have haunted me, all the unresolved issues in my life, have existed in a narrows that I have traveled with careful steps. There was no way out except backward or forward, yet the path has always been one I chose rather than one assigned to me. These journeys presented the most exciting experiences of my life, those that I would not trade ever for a hot shower, enchiladas, and a soft bed. Yet I bear the scars of these escapades as surely as my bruised ankles and cut, rubbery legs from Zion Canyon. They are the images that still haunt me when I am waking or asleep.

One hundred years from now we will all be dead. What difference does it make what I do in my lifetime or what you or anyone else does? Who cares whether I spent this or any day hiking the narrows or lying in bed staring at the ceiling fan?

Each day, I get out of bed and proceed to do all of the things that I usually do—groom myself, say goodbye to my wife before she heads off to work, take my son to school, commute to the university, attend meetings, talk to people, write a little, teach a little, talk on the phone, head home, spend time with my family, all the things that seem so important at the time. And every day brings some sort of crisis. Someone has been mean to me; my feelings are hurt. Two people want different things, so they lock horns until one emerges the victor. Somebody is upset about something that is believed to be unjust. Just the usual assortment of human conflict and negotiation.

I wonder if anything that I do really matters. I delude myself with the notion that my work is important, that I am on a noble quest to help people. I desperately want to believe that the pain and suffering I have lived through have some useful purpose, that my daily actions are of some lasting use. At first, it is easy to entertain this fantasy. Students stop by to thank me for some kindness; I can quite often see the dawn of some understanding on their faces when I explain some previously incomprehensible idea. Ex-clients sometimes call to tell me how well they are doing. Surely this must mean that I am doing something important.

But as hard as I work to make a dent in the world, to leave something behind as a remnant of my existence, I am not altogether convinced that this is a worthwhile enterprise. I am haunted by the drive to own things, and then am stuck paying for them. I am so concerned with what I want to do next that I miss what is happening right now.

I stop. Look around. This whole inner dialogue took place as I was walking through one of the most beautiful places on earth. As the walls loom skyward, closing in my view, blocking out the light, I look inward. With each step I take, I feel myself move backward in time. I consider how I got to this point in the journey, just as I wonder about how I grew to be a therapist.

I take a step. And another. Feel the rain on my face. Touch the slick walls. Smell the water. Ignore the pain. Remember to breathe. Study the rapids. Plan the next step, maybe even the one after that. This walk through the narrows is a journey taken to forget my doubts and uncertainties. What I know for sure is that I am tired and cold, hungry, frightened, and sore. I have one foot in the present, the step of a sturdy adult, and another in the past, the uncertain lurch of a lost child.

3

Recruited as a Child

A s I journey back into time, leaving the beauty of my present surroundings for the bleakness of the past, I wonder how I ended up where I am now. How and why did I ever become a therapist and not an entrepreneur like my brothers, a salesman like my father, or a printer like my grandfather?

Why People Become Therapists

There are many reasons why someone might become a professional helper. I have known colleagues who became therapists because they thought it was easier than being a client; they had issues they needed to work on and thought that, with proper training, they could do it themselves. There are others who thrive on power. They are afraid and yet are drawn to closeness with others, especially when they can be in control. Being a therapist allows them to get as close to another human being as is possible, with minimal risk. Furthermore, it can feel good to know that other people's lives hang in the balance of what the therapist says and does.

Other therapists I have known chose this profession because of the status and reverence it generates. People believe that we can read minds, that we know "truth," that we can see things that are invisible to mere mortals. We are admired as wise and witty sages (when we are not being resented and mocked for all that we pretend to do but cannot deliver).

Still others do not feel that they had a choice as to what they would do in later life. They were "trained" as children to be rescuers and mediators within their own families. They learned quite early how to distract parents from battles, how to patch up hostilities between siblings, or how to bring comfort to those suffering greatly. Of course, such battlefield heroics do not come without certain risks and often result in deep wounds for the one who is trying to help.

Ask any therapist you know why he or she picked this career, and it is likely you will hear this pat answer, "Because I like to help people." I don't deny that liking to help *is* part of the motive for most who become therapists, even if it is hardly the whole picture. But I know that I must also reluctantly admit that each of the previous motives played a part in my own choice. I enjoy the power and one-way intimacy of getting close to people without having to risk much of myself in the process. I like the deference that people show me, the uneasiness they feel, as if I could read their minds and uncover their secrets. I like being a know-it-all. However, I was also one of those who did not have much choice.

My Parents' Keeper

The eldest of three children, I was recruited quite early into the role of helper. My parents did not like one another very well and were quite vocal about their feelings. Inevitably, my mother would end up drunk, and my father would storm out of the house. Or my father would flee, and *then* my mother would lock herself in her room.

My mother was sandwiched between her father, who emotionally abused her, and my father, who neglected her. She was overmatched and overwhelmed by three active sons who were continuously at each other's throats. When she would retreat into her bedroom with her scotch, Valium, and chocolate, we would take over the house, at least during daylight hours. At night, our home became a place of tears.

I can vividly recall some of the phone conversations I had at age twelve with my mother's therapist late at night: "Doctor, my mom took some pills and had too much to drink. She told me to take care of my brothers after she is gone. I'm scared. I don't know what to do." I carefully took down his instructions, the budding therapist in training: See if I can wake her. Stay with her until a friend arrives. Tell her when her next appointment is.

Needless to say, I became accustomed to trying to help other people survive. Since I was such a lousy student and so uninspired, without talent as an athlete or scholar, at least I felt useful as a rescuer. Maybe I couldn't catch fly balls, dribble a basketball, or make sense of my math books, but at least I had a useful purpose. I could help others.

A lost child, I was recruited to help others find their way. At first, I had been the designated "problem" in our family—as long as I was in trouble, academically or socially, my parents seemed to stop arguing long enough to figure out what to do with me. I can still hear them whispering behind a closed door on the day I brought home my report card. Whatever would they do with me? Some of my parent-teacher conferences occupy my fondest memories—these meetings were the only places I ever remember going where both my parents would show up at the same time.

My parents' arguments became more and more frequent. Then there was a period of eery silence. Each retreated into a personal world, my mother behind the bedroom door and my father out onto the golf course. I recall the day my father moved out of the house to escape my mother's unhappiness and continue a life on his own. For hours, I sat crying in his closet with the door closed as I cradled a pair of shoes that he had left behind. I counted the tiny holes on his wing tips and wondered what I would do when the time came for me to leave the closet.

A few therapists since that time have ventured that I must have felt very angry towards my father, abandoning us like that. Resentful? I envied him. I thought, "Take me. Please, take me with you."

My mother told me I was now the man of the house. I would have to help her take care of things. I wondered if my brothers would have to listen to me.

I was my mother's designated confidante: "Your father is no good. . . . I don't want you talking to him anymore about anything that happens in this house. He's made his own bed [with my mother's best friend], so let him lie in it."

I was my parents' go-between: "Tell your mother that I will pick you guys up on Sunday." "Tell your father he will have to make other arrangements." "Tell your mother to call me." They didn't talk much on the phone as long as they had me to speak through.

In my role as the responsible male in the house, I was also my brothers' keeper, the one to whom the younger ones could turn. In this, I did a fairly lousy job. I teased my brothers mercilessly and ruled them through intimidation and guile. I was just acting like any eldest child my age, but my days as just a kid were now past. Even though I felt so lost myself, I was expected to grow up quickly, to be a therapist long before I ever received any formal training.

4

Reliving My Past

I am well aware of the distortion that takes place in writing personal history. We only have to compare our versions of events with the perceptions of others to find there are many different realities.

It has been said that there are no happy childhoods, only fond memories that become embellished over time. Certainly from the perspective of a child, the daily events of life—a skinned knee, a teacher's remark, a parent's censure, a disappointment—do take on dramatic proportions. To a little person, every little happening can seem gargantuan, and these events can also swell in importance once our adult minds get hold of them and play with them a bit.

I recall one of my brothers reporting to me a few years ago about the work he had been doing with a therapist. He had just had a major insight: the reason he had struggled throughout his life with addictions and intimacy was that he had been abandoned not only by his father but by his older brother (me), and left to take care of his alcoholic mother without help since the critical age of twelve. It was a great theory, one that he and his therapist were especially proud of.

The only problem with it was that it was based on some fictional assumptions. During our conversation, I hesitantly mentioned to him that, in fact, I had not moved out of the house until I was a senior in high school, when he was fifteen not twelve. "Oh," he replied with nervous laughter. "Are you sure about that? I remember . . ."

Ah, yes, the things we remember.

I have to acknowledge that my memories, too, have *got* to be distorted, even exaggerated, including recollections of the events that helped shape me as a therapist. It is not that my early life was so traumatic as much as it *felt* that way to me, both at the time and later.

I was neither abused nor neglected as a child. My parents did the best they could with what they had at the time. I no longer hold any resentments or, for that matter, wish that things could have been any different. Now a parent myself, I know how hard it is to do that job in such a way that I am not filled with regrets for what I might have done otherwise. Nevertheless, I did (and do) experience quite a bit of pain as an aftermath to what I lived through as a child. These things were not done *to* me as much as I was caught in the cross fire of the things some people were doing to themselves and one another.

Nobody Noticed I Could Not See

Not too long ago I was sitting in a chair, dozing a bit, thinking about being a kid. I remembered a job I had working as a caddie at the Detroit Golf Club. It was supposed to be some kind of big deal since I was the first Jew there. I recall feeling a lot of pressure to do well.

What I remember most about this time in my life is how I could never see the damn golf balls after they were hit. Here it was my job to spot the balls after the golfers took their swings, and I could never find them once they took off into the air. I never told anyone this. I just assumed there was some technique to ball spotting, some special skill that I had yet to master. This kind of behavior, faking it until I could figure out what was going on, became a major theme in my life. Look as if I know what I am doing. Head in the direction all the others are going. Act as if it is *their* fault they can't see their own damn ball. Later, this was for a while the hallmark to me of the ideal posture for a therapist.

This image of not being able to see triggers another recollection that embodies a significant part of my childhood. I remember sitting in math class daydreaming, staring out the window at the promise of freedom. I was lost in my own world, oblivious to whatever was going on around me, that is at least until my knee accidently bumped the back of the girl sitting in front of me. Then I would lose myself in a different sort of fantasy, one that transported me to another . . . "Jeffrey! *Jeffrey Kottler!* Perhaps you can tell us how $20x - 5x^2 = 0$?"

Yeah, sure. Whenever the teacher would call on me, I never knew the answer. I would mumble something under my breath and stare out the window, waiting for her to move on to someone else she could humiliate. The reason I could not, in my wildest dreams, venture a reasonable guess to the teacher's question is that I could never see what was on the board. It was all a blurry haze to me.

Yet a third image I have is of sitting at a football game with my father. I hated going to those games. It was cold. Completely boring. The Lions rarely won. I would stare off into the crowds. My Dad would yell at me for not seeing a certain great play: "Didn't you see that run? I don't know why I even bring you to these games if you aren't going to pay attention!"

The truth is, as I just this moment realized, that I couldn't see a damn thing as a kid. Ever. I never knew this, of course, because a blurry nearsighted world was normal to me. I couldn't see a golf ball, a blackboard, or even a football field. I couldn't see a baseball. Playing right field, I used to miss fly balls because I couldn't see them until it was too late. Weighing my self-esteem like any young boy by my ability to hit a tiny ball whizzing by with a skinny stick, I didn't have a chance.

What amazes me is that throughout most of my childhood I was half-blind, and my parents never noticed. Neither did my teachers. Did they not see that I held books too close to my face, or that I sat right in front of the television? I seriously wonder what effect my poor vision had on my development, my sense of competence as a child. When I finally got glasses (an optometrist married into the family), the good doctor had a theory that a weak prescription would force my eyes to get stronger. The first year I had my driver's license, I was in five separate accidents. I was probably telling the truth when I kept claiming that I couldn't see the other cars. (My orthodontist also had a theory. He thought that by straightening my baby teeth, my permanent teeth would grow in straight. I had perfect baby teeth, but when they fell out my new teeth still grew in crooked, and I wore braces for five years.)

Between my braces, bumping into walls, striking out a lot, and not seeing much of what was going on in school (or anywhere else), I was not in the best of shape, self-esteemwise. I finally escaped that past only to find that now, as a father with my own child, I am haunted by flashbacks to these experiences.

What Goes Around . . .

My mother was mostly out of the picture during my childhood. She was chronically depressed and unhappy most of her life; after my parents divorced, she slipped even deeper into an alcoholic haze. I turned to my father for support but he wasn't around very much. By the time he was available to me, I resented him terribly—because I had to share him with my brothers and his new wife, because he was perfect in everything he did, because try as I might, I could not knock him off his pedestal. He was everything I was not—remarkably handsome, socially charming, athletic, confident, and popular.

We battled to a point where we reached an uneasy truce. It became a guiding force of my life that I would excel in areas that were out of his reach. He was a champion golfer, bridge and backgammon player, and a gambler with remarkable success at the gin tables. I chose, instead, a different field to play in, one that my father does not understand to this day. It is because I have tried so hard to be different, to carve out my own territory, that we get along. That and the stroke he had several years ago that among its devastating effects made him more dependent but also more affectionate and human.

From this account, you may be able to see with far more clarity than I ever could the glimmerings of what nudged me, ever so slowly and inexorably, in the direction of being a therapist. I was insecure, uncoordinated, and unsure of myself. I was committed to one thing in life, that was taking care of my mother. Even there, however, I was doing by my own admission a poor job—fighting with my brothers, messing up in school, acting weird and moody.

I desperately wanted to excel in something, but I could never come close to what I perceived were my father's high expectations. I would never be as handsome or charming or gregarious or popular as he was. Perhaps, just perhaps, I could get into an area that was all my own, one in which I would not have to compete with him or anyone else. To do so, however, meant that I would have to get used to being and feeling alone. That I was already pretty good at.

Part II

Skeptical Student

5

Alone in the Dark

I have always felt like an outsider, so different from other people. When my friends were interested in sports, I sat alone in my room and played the guitar. I couldn't sing or even keep a tune, but I found solace alone in the dark. I have already mentioned how I retreated inside myself while my classmates did their homework or dutifully paid attention in class. There was nothing profound in these reveries. I might catch a glimpse of a girl's bra when she lifted up her arm to answer a question, and then I was gone for the rest of the hour.

It was my deepest fear that others would discover how strange I was. I did my best to fit in, but invariably I slipped up. Not knowing my peers' unwritten dress codes, I wore white socks to school and suffered weeks of harassment. Most of the time, I had no idea what was going on in class. I would stare at algebraic equations on the board through my new glasses, trying to figure out what they meant, or even what they were for. Most of all, I was afraid of the dark. I slept with a night-light. Once, I saw *The Wax Museum*, a movie in which a character lay down in a canopy bed only to glance up and see the blade of a guillotine slicing down, through his neck. I slept in a canopy bed. Forever after, I slept with my head at the foot of the bed. I figured if there were a guillotine waiting for me, I would cheat it by giving up my feet but not my head.

As I grew older, my fears of the dark transposed into other worries.

Still convinced that deep down inside I was crazy as a loon, I tried to fit in as best I could. I must have developed some endearing qualities because, while for most of my life people have said to me, "Kottler, you're crazy!" they say it affectionately.

I hoped my study of psychology would help me find my way out of this inner darkness, as I was finding my way out of my fear of literal darkness. If only I could discover the origins of all my other fears, perhaps I might find some comfort in my aloneness. I became fascinated with deviance; I even wrote a thesis on the subject. I had a theory that strange people were just misunderstood. I found consolation in the blurred boundaries between creativity and madness. I just knew that some day I was going to go off the deep end, and I was doing all the preparation I could to cushion the fall.

I fought going into the military not because I was afraid to go to Vietnam but because I didn't think that my fragile identity would make it through boot camp. Give me a rifle and send me into the jungle? Fine. I'm willing. But shave my head and strip away my individuality? That I could never have survived. Therefore my first experience of seeing a therapist occurred during my efforts to win an exemption from military service by reason of insanity. "Look Doc," I explained. "I am probably not crazy. Yet. But put me in that confined place, and I will make everyone's life miserable." The psychiatrist readily agreed, a little too quickly for my own comfort.

This only confirmed my suspicions that I really was different. Even an expert thought so. It was at this point that I grew to enjoy living in the dark. Maybe I was lost, wandering aimlessly, but I felt safe enough—nobody could hurt me.

Stumbling into a Profession

My entry into therapy as a profession was hardly a linear progression of deliberate, conscious choices. When I first enrolled in college, I had selected business administration because that was what my father thought was best. Making money was the standard of success in my family. Indeed, I started out my early adulthood determined that I would accomplish that goal. This resolve lasted fifteen minutes into the very first orientation session for business majors. I could not help but notice that there were no females present. What kind of fun would college (or life) be if I had to spend it only in the company of men?

I bolted the room and started wandering the halls. I noticed one session in particular that had more than its fair distribution of young women. "So *that's* where they went," I mused, as if there were some conspiracy to deprive me further of opportunities for female companionship (my adolescence had not provided me with much experience). I entered that classroom with only one thought in mind, "This is where the girls are."

I am utterly embarrassed to admit that this was the initial impetus that led me into psychology, or at least, that got my attention long enough to hint to me I had not only found my calling but also a way to heal myself. I would like to believe that, eventually, I would have found my way anyway. There is no doubt, however, that my first priority in life at that time was trying to make sense of relationships between men and women, in particular so that I might some day find a female person whom I might understand and who would understand me in return.

I was delighted to discover that psychology was incredibly interesting, even apart from the stimulating companionship of my classmates. Since I was too shy to actually approach anyone, I settled for a very active fantasy life plus this first real interest in anything remotely academic. I studied the subject as if my life depended on it, and in one sense, it did. I could not believe that there was a discipline that had as its primary mission the goal of trying to understand why people behave the way they do. Finally, I could try to make sense of what had been happening in my life. I could figure out why I was so different from others. I could learn what it was about me that others might find likeable.

Being Paid to Read Books

Being a college student, especially a skeptical one, allowed me to test the boundaries of being different. Since my parents had never gone to college, I was in new territory for my family. They didn't understand what I was doing, the stuff I was reading, the ideas in my head.

It did not come to me all at once but in little pieces that maybe I could sit where I could observe others stumbling through the dark. Perhaps I might even be of use, having had so much experience feeling lost. Certainly, I would not feel so alone if I were listening to other people struggle with their own demons. Walking among the wounded, I would not seem so strange. Besides, people have different standards for therapists: we are allowed to be eccentric; it gives us character.

I discovered, to my relief, that I wasn't the only one seeking reassurance that he or she was sane by training to be a therapist. Many of my fellow students had been wounded as well—crippled emotionally as children by alcoholic, abusive, or neglectful parents. I may still have been in the dark, but I wasn't alone.

I also knew at this point that I loved being a student. It was like being at summer camp all year round. My only job in life was to read books and talk about ideas, listening to interesting people speak with passion about what gave their lives meaning. This was not work, and if I could figure out a way to avoid having to get a real job I was going to do it, since I had already tried every grungy job in existence—from assembly-line worker and printer's apprentice to busboy and envelope stuffer. It occurred to me that being a teacher, a professor, or a therapist (whom I thought of as a private tutor in lessons of life) would allow me to continue in the role of skeptical student. I could continue to read books and, in a sense, get paid for doing so. Furthermore, as I have noted, being different is considered an asset in these professions.

I saw another advantage as well. Like most people who gravitate to the counseling profession, I thought I was entering a "social" discipline. After all, with its roots in education and the *social* sciences, with its distinctly interpersonal, helpful nature, I believed that counseling would provide not only a career but a home. So, hungry for companionship, understanding, and acceptance by like-minded folks, I joyously began graduate school and my training under the assumption I would never feel alone again.

Going into Training

When I started it, I did not realize the extent to which training to be a therapist would strengthen me personally. The mentors I had read about—Freud, Jung, and others—may have been brilliant theoreticians, researchers, and clinicians, but they surely did not seem like very fully functioning individuals. I was particularly distressed to learn about Freud's petty jealousies, his cocaine and cigar addictions, his messiah complex. Heck, the guy gave up sex when he was *my* age! And this was my hero? This was the man who invented therapy?

The other leaders in the field did not seem significantly better adjusted. Since most of my teachers and mentors were brilliant at talking but less skilled at putting their beliefs into practice, I did not expect personal growth to come with the territory. I believed that I would forever be impaired but that at least my pain could help others find their way into the light. It was with profound amazement that I observed my confidence and personal control improve as I learned the skills of helping. Privy to the secrets of others, I realized that I never had been alone in the dark; I just had kept my eyes closed.

Learning to *be* a therapist is a curious undertaking. The official skill development is perhaps the easiest part of all. Acquiring the discrete set of generic behaviors common to all practitioners, regardless of their orientation, involves learning the diagnostic system for assessing client complaints, and mastering the skills of questioning, reflection, interpretation, and confrontation. Then there are the other, more subtle skills that require study and practice—using self-disclosure appropriately, reframing problems in ways they can more easily be solved, guiding people in directions that are supposed to be good for them.

All in all, the graduate school portion of learning to be a therapist was remarkably boring. Everything was arranged according to the classes we attended, as if by going to these rooms at particular times, taking tests, and writing papers, we would be deemed worthy of joining the exclusive club. I was trying so hard to prove myself, to win my professors' approval, to earn perfect grades, I forgot to concentrate on learning anything that might be useful to me later. School was simply a place where I earned enough credits to get a degree.

I did have some amazing relationships with a few of my professors who mentored me in a big way. They recognized something in my writing voice and my interpersonal style that seemed worthwhile to nurture along. It was informal experiences with them that taught me the most at that time about being a therapist. In relationships that would now be considered gross breaches of ethical conduct because of the multiple roles that were involved, I was treated to rare glimpses into the inner workings of therapeutic life. One of my professors simultaneously acted in my life as a teacher, supervisor, therapist, friend, and collaborator. As confusing as these different, contradictory roles became, I will forever feel grateful for how open and giving this fellow was, at least until we tried to relate to one another as equals.

I also spent one year in a counseling group with this professor. I learned more about how to do therapy by being a client than I ever did in supervision or the classroom. I had the opportunity to observe firsthand how this master worked wonders with our group's intertwined lives. I noted what got to me and what didn't. I practiced stuff that I had been learning, imitated him whenever I could, noted instant feedback with the other group members, seeing what worked and what didn't for them. Most of all, I was invited into this man's life. He was a surrogate father to me, an ideal teacher, a confidante, counselor, and friend. I stopped trying to make sense of what these multiple roles were all about and went with the flow. I just opened myself up to whatever he offered, read the books he introduced me to, followed his leads, and took his advice without question.

This mentor relationship, which lasted almost a decade, ultimately ended in abrupt silence which, to this day, I do not understand. One day, I received a letter from him informing me that he would rather not have much else to do with me. As is the case with most conflicted relationships, we had each blamed one another for the relationship's problems. He felt that I was too judgmental and intolerant of him, that I had sold out for the good life once I moved to suburbia. I felt that his occasional drunken, irresponsible, sometimes abusive behavior was simply not acceptable. In spite of our difficulties in the way this relationship ended, it had been the primary ground out of which I initially developed as a therapist.

One aspect of my training years that was certainly worth putting up with all the other stuff was the structured internship experiences. Everyone should have the opportunity to sit in a room with someone in pain, knowing that your supervisor and peers are watching from behind one-way mirrors, that cameras are recording every move and microphones are picking up every sound. Both the best and the worst part is reviewing the tapes afterwards, having every single mistake and misjudgment (of which there will be dozens in a session with even the most accomplished practitioner) pointed out to you in such a way that you will not repeat them.

I found quite early that I was pretty good at doing therapy. The pain of my own childhood had sensitized me to the anguish of others. My own vulnerability comes through in sessions in such a way that it invites reciprocal trust, just as I suppose it does in my writing. I am a warm, friendly sort of person; this helps people to open up as well, and also to forgive me when I mess up. In spite of, or perhaps because of, my being a skeptical student, people feel reassured that I will tell them truth.

Receiving Unexpected Dividends

There were some benefits in my training that I had not anticipated. As I learned to listen more carefully and respond more sensitively, I found my personal relationships improving dramatically. It was as if I had learned the secrets of the universe—with practice, I *could* read minds and get people to like me.

In time, I learned how to make most anyone feel comfortable. I could ask great questions and get quickly to the essence of things. I learned how to think more clearly and help others to do the same. I became quite skilled at confronting people in ways that they actually felt grateful for. I could see and hear things that were invisible to others; more importantly, I was not afraid to tell the truth. I felt such incredible power!

I remember one of my first clients in graduate school, a professor at the university where I was doing my internship. He was in awful pain, depressed, despondent, even suicidal, and here he was looking to me for answers. I couldn't believe that I had reached a stage in my life (now all of twenty-four years) in which smart people looked to me for ways to help them out of the dark.

Best of all, I learned that there were a heck of a lot of people walking around who were much stranger than I was. Clients would tell me the secrets of their bizarre lives—sucking toes, *with* socks on; romancing cows; leading double lives.

And the more I heard, the better I felt.

At the same time, I observed that many of my supervisors, although apparently successful as professionals, could barely keep their own lives together. I knew therapists who routinely slept with their clients, defrauded insurance companies, and manipulated others for their own gain. I saw marriage counselors who could not sustain intimate relationships in their own lives. It seemed that although we therapists were not unusually disturbed, we had at least our fair share of emotional cripples, and I wondered how it was possible for us to do this kind of work and not practice on ourselves what we asked others to do.

I resolved that I would devote my life to being a therapist. I would not act all together only when the meter was running and I had an audience watching. I would try my absolute hardest to be what I tried to help others to be. I would apply all the skills and knowledge at my disposal to help myself.

Since therapists are, by and large, a gregarious bunch, I believed training for this profession would help me to find my way out of a life-long shell of shyness and isolation. As a student and as an intern, I felt part of a larger community of people who shared similar values, interests, and aspirations. This gave me another way to escape feeling that I was finding my way alone in the dark; now I would have the company of others with whom I could hold hands.

Little did I realize what a solitary form of work I had chosen. I quickly learned that whereas I might work in the company of others, I rarely had time to *talk* to them. My fellow students and I were always busy doing things that seemed so important. When we were together, most of our time was spent "getting things done," fighting for our individual agendas, "being productive." A quick hug or superficial "How's it going?" left me feeling even more frustrated than no communication at all.

As I continued to grow from a fledgling intern into a licensed professional, I was disturbed that this sense of isolation only grew worse. My office sometimes felt like a cave where I would sit all day seeing a stream of people come in to tell their stories, beg for relief, and then move out into the world. Their lives were often deeply interesting but also excruciatingly painful. I would listen. I would do my best to respond helpfully. Most of all, I would keep everything to myself. Then I was alone not only with my own fears and inadequacies but everyone else's as well!

It is now many years later, and I have certainly profited from all the solitary reflective time that results from keeping other people's secrets. It was these clients who ultimately helped me find my way through the dark, not my teachers and supervisors. As I listened to their stories, I did not feel so alone. As the intimacy in these relationships grew, it seemed to fill a void in me that provided the experience and the confidence to reach out to others. I became a student of other people's lives. Instead of reading books, I now expanded my repertoire to learn as much as I could from the mistakes that others make.

There was, however, that lingering problem of working so much in isolation. If I had understood the extent to which my essential aloneness would be intensified when I became a therapist, I would have become a farmer or truck driver instead. I never realized the extent to which therapists have so little time to be with, and to help, one another. The clock is always running. There are clients to see, meetings to attend, paperwork to catch up on, phone calls to return. But so little time to talk to anyone who is not a client.

We therapists each sit alone in our offices. The conventions of our practice prevent interruptions. We are cut off from friends, family, and the outside world once we are in session. We are prohibited from discussing what we do, except during designated moments. We are sometimes so busy juggling our various roles and responsibilities, we hardly notice that not only has night fallen outside but that much of the time we are also sitting in yet another form of darkness. Often we don't know what to do with a client; we can barely make sense of what is happening to the person. Yet we must bear the responsibilities that are part of every decision we make.

As we proceed, lost, alone, tripping over obstacles we cannot even identify, much less avoid, clients cling to us, pleading that we shed some light on their paths. Supervisors call out to us to move faster. And sometimes we wonder if we are not just going in circles, around and around, doomed to spend all eternity in the dark.

6

Feeling Useful

Being in a student role is not exactly conducive to feeling powerful. Students are peons, forced to beg and grovel, to be deferential, to jump through hoops. Other people make decisions about where you have to be, and what you do when you get there. You may be forced to watch a film, participate in some discussion, or listen to whatever the professor decides that he or she wants to talk about that day. Through it all, you have to take notes, anticipate what you might be expected to remember, and be prepared to spit it back on demand.

Needless to say, being a student was not much fun for me. In spite of the opportunities to learn, I hated having my life held in the hands of anyone else, especially someone who had the power to decide if I was worthy or not. I fought back whenever I could, but I also felt torn because I was so dependent on their good opinions of me: "Should I disagree with him, or do I risk alienating him? If I do speak my mind, maybe he will respect me more." I hated myself for this spineless approval seeking and despised the structure that forced me to sit still for so long in the same place. When you are student, you can't even go to the bathroom when you want.

Peak Experiences

But in spite of the disagreeable features of the student role, I quite liked the result that was developing in me. For one of the few times in my life, I felt as though what I was doing was truly important. The worthiness of my life, perhaps *any* life, is measured in terms of how much good is accomplished. This has nothing to do with earning brownie points to gain entrance into heaven; it has to do with our ability to live with ourselves, because we are the ones who do the measuring.

To this day, I assess the value of who I am according to the good I have created for others. There are days when I feel so useful I walk on air. I *know*, beyond a shadow of a doubt, that I have helped another human being. This person may not even have been a client, a student, a reader, or a therapist I am supervising. Sometimes I have been most useful to perfect strangers. Following through on my commitment to be what I try to help others to be, I walk around this Earth trying to be as nice to people as I possibly can.

A number of images flash through my mind when I recall the magical moments of my life. There are some critical experiences that seem relatively predicable—when I first met the woman who would become my wife, when my son was born, and when I skied alone on a glacier. But the other peak experiences that stand out are those that meet my need to feel useful and in which, as a result of my efforts, I know I did some good for someone else, either in a session or in one of those spontaneous altruistic moments where my being at the right place at the right time allowed me to do something that made a difference.

For example, I was driving down a street when, out of the corner of my eye, I caught a glimpse of movement that seemed, somehow, incongruent with the surroundings. I don't know why I pulled over to the side of the road, but I felt some sense of urgency. Cars were whooshing by, their unconcerned occupants focused on their destinations. But I momentarily forgot where I was headed. Before me I saw someone, or something, in distress.

As I approached this erratically moving object, it took shape as a motorized wheelchair, hiccupping back and forth, stuck on some gravel. Strapped inside was a child who appeared completely para-lyzed except for the single digit that was trying to operate the chair in these adverse circumstances. We eyed each other warily, each of us breathing hard, the child from exertion, and me from apprehension about what I was facing. It had immediately become apparent that this child was in trouble. Here she was alone in a field, trapped on some gravel, and unable to free herself from the predicament. She seemed to be making some noise, a guttural grunting sound, but as I tried to communicate with her, I couldn't tell if she was asking for help or warning me to stay way. I felt almost as helpless and frustrated as she was. I kept saying over and over, "Can I help you? Can I help you?" to which she would attempt to fling her body around and grunt incomprehensibly. I did not know where she had come from or where she was going. Cars kept speeding by. I sat down next to her on the ground and started crying in exasperation. I wanted to help, but I did not know what to do.

After both of us calmed down, the girl was able to slowly, laboriously, feed me a phone number. Elated with our progress, I ran to a phone booth after reassuring her I would return. While we waited for a van to come and get her (she had wandered off from a school several blocks away), I sat at her feet and spoke to her soothingly, saying that everything would be all right. She grunted back in her own way, perhaps reassuring me as well.

It has been years since this incident occurred, yet my mind returns to it again and again. There have been other times when I have been privileged to be helpful to someone else, when I have employed my skills as therapist or teacher or writer, and never have I felt more useful than in those moments. It seems as if my whole life is redeemed by the opportunity to help someone else, as if my whole existence is defined by what I do that is good. I think of these gestures as valuable nuggets I can scatter throughout the world, or that small slice of it of which I am a part. If I can smile at someone and make him or her feel good for a moment, if I can do or say something that makes a difference in someone's life, then I feel as if all the effort I have devoted to healing myself has some larger purpose and meaning.

What Matters Most

I struggled with such feelings of exhilaration during my training years. I felt uncomfortable with the power and pleasure of holding other people's welfare in my hands. On the one hand, I disliked the burden of responsibility. It was difficult for me to like and respect people who were helpless and refused to do anything to change their situations, although I could feel pity, perhaps even compassion, for them. On the other hand, I came to recognize that the parts of them I had difficulty with were the same things that I most despised in myself. It was like seeing my mother's despair in the eyes of every client I tried to help. Still a beginner in my profession, I was neither prepared nor able to separate my need to feel useful from the client's need for understanding and caring.

I was finding the relationships I developed with my first clients to be very strange. Here I was, learning the most personal details of their lives—the secrets and the shame, the hidden and unconscious motives and the most private compartments. And yet these people knew next to nothing about me. Each client and I became almost as close as two people can be, but I didn't risk much in the process. When a client did not like me, I could say it was my job not to be liked. If that did not work, I could try on for size the reasoning that I was just getting too close to the essence of things, and the client couldn't handle it. I was never rejected as a person; people fled when I did my job a little too well. Or so I told myself.

I told clients that I refused to be responsible for their decisions and their lives. I would not tolerate dependency in most any form. When a client thanked me for being helpful, I did not graciously accept his or her gratitude; I emphasized that *he* did the work or that *she* was the one who succeeded or failed.

But I didn't believe this for a minute. Feeling unimportant and useless, my essential validation as a human being has come from others who acknowledge that my efforts have been appreciated. My life on Earth accrues meaning only in terms of what I have done and those whom I have most recently helped. To this day, as I drift off to sleep at night, sometimes my last conscious thought is a pointed question. As I walk along the narrows, I ask myself: How have I been useful? What I have done that really matters?

7

The Absurdity of What I Do

As a skeptical student, I had my doubts and suspicions about the field I had recently joined. I was probably not the most beloved member of my classes. I may have had love, compassion, and the desire to help in my heart, but I was cynical about some obvious paradoxes in what it is that therapists do.

I looked, for example, at this relationship that we develop with our clients, this alliance that is supposed to be healing, and I was struck by a number of absurdities. How is it that this therapeutic relationship is supposed to be permissive and open when it is actually structured and contrived? We act as if the client can do or say whatever she likes, but we really have lots of rules regarding what is appropriate and what is not:

- Be grateful to me, but not so much so that you appear dependent.

- Be deferential but not obsequious.

- Say whatever you want but don't interrupt me.

- Talk about feelings, not analytical observations (let *me* do that).

- Arrive on time and leave promptly.

- Tell me your secrets—make them juicy and interesting.

- Don't blame other people for the predicaments you find yourself in.

- Speak in the language of therapy, rich with symbols and metaphors.

This relationship is supposed to be genuinely caring, yet when the client walks out of the room, she often ceases to exist in our minds. It is supposed to be safe and comforting, yet we often ask clients to do very risky things. We are purportedly fostering independence in clients, yet we do so in such a way that they become temporarily dependent on us. We pretend that this relationship is intimate and personal, yet it is actually professional and distant, sometimes even quite manipulative in imposing therapists' hidden agendas.

You get the picture. Now imagine that I expressed these absurdities I had found to all those who would listen. As I said, I was not the easiest student to have around. And deep down inside, I did not have much faith in what I was doing. In some ways, believing in therapy is like believing in the tooth fairy—both are based on faith.

Therapy is essentially built on the belief system of both participants. If I am sure that what I have to offer is going to be helpful, and I can convince you that this is true, then most whatever I do is going to work in some ways. This includes not only whether I choose to help you alone or in the context of your family or a group of strangers but also whether I decide to concentrate on your feelings, thoughts, or behavior; to mostly listen or to talk a lot; to have you talk or draw pictures, chant on a hilltop, or dance into exhaustion; to focus on the meaning behind your behavior or change the behavior itself; or to work with you over a few weeks or several years.

One of the thoughts that haunts me the most is the realization that if I take a few steps back from what I do for a living and look at the work critically, I cannot with any confidence understand what is going on, nor why it works. I know this sounds surprising for someone who has written a dozen books that are supposed to help practitioners improve the quality of their work or to teach beginners how to do this complicated business. It is just that sometimes the whole process seems like a big hoax to me, not one that we are putting over on the public, but on ourselves.

Automobile mechanics understand the human capacity for doubt all too well. When some mysterious ailment befalls our vehicle we take it in to a garage for repairs. We hope that when we return a few hours later, the problem will be fixed, and the service manager will explain what was wrong and what was done to rectify it. Then we will be handed a bill that details the number of hours the job took and a list of parts that were used. This is all very impressive. Moreover, since mechanics know that many people are utterly befuddled by the workings of an automobile and that, further, they are mistrustful that others might be taking advantage of them, mechanics supply extra proof that they did what they said they did.

As you drive away, tentatively, critically listening for the same symptoms that brought you in, you can not help but notice that on the floor on the passenger side is a jumbled pile of old, greasy metal pieces. These are the offending parts that were removed. If we know how to do an autopsy on them, if we recognize where each part came from and what it is supposed to look like when it is working properly, it is theoretically possible for us to reconstruct what went wrong, thereby providing physical evidence for the explanation that we were given. The effect of such physical manifestation of proof is the same even when we look dumbly on as the mechanic points to some piece of rubber, chuckles loudly to himself, and says, "Yup, *that* is your problem. Gasket's gone bad." Now, we may not know what a gasket is, what it is supposed to do, and why it went bad, but there it is before us—*proof* that the mechanic's explanation holds merit.

Of course, mechanics can provide physical proof precisely because their work differs from that of the therapists in critical respects. Cars are hardly as complex as the human mind and body, yet when I compare the experience of consulting a mechanic to what happens when a person seeks my services, I can only shake my head in wonder. The experience starts off similarly. Someone comes in with some problem in need of fixing. But after I ask a few questions to determine what is wrong, things change radically. Whereas a mechanic will give me a fairly accurate prediction of what the costs will be, and even tell me when the job will be done (give or take an hour or two), I say to my client, "Well, it all depends." Furthermore, I say this with the assurance that such vagueness is normal and customary.

I am trying to imagine how I would react to a mechanic who told me what I would tell him if he came to see me:

Well, you have had this problem for some time, and furthermore, this isn't the first time this has happened to you. I will need to get a lot more background information about the other cars you have driven. Perhaps you could tell me what it was like for you the first time you saw a car? What about when you first saw this one? . . .

I can't tell you exactly how long this job will take. A lot depends on you. I might be able to fix you up in a few minutes; then again it could take years. It may seem like a simple valve adjustment on the surface, but other items may be lurking inside; you may need a complete overhaul. I've got a space available on Thursday at 3:00. That will be *every* Thursday until we get to the bottom of this. Please pay the receptionist on your way out. . . .

How are you going to drive your car under these conditions until it is fixed? Hey, that's not *my* problem; *you* are the one who let things get this bad. If only your pride had not kept you from asking for help. Look, I don't mean to be harsh, but this is going to take some time. You have lived with this car for years and know it intimately, and *you* can't figure out what is wrong. How am I supposed to figure it out in a mere hour?

I don't think I would react happily on hearing this or feel much confidence in the mechanic.

Not only can I not give my clients an accurate prediction of how long their "service" will take, but most of the time I don't really know what the problem is. I do have some rough ideas, of course. Some of the time, I even feel fairly confident in my explanations. But by "fairly confident," I mean simply better than chance. This is why I am so terrified of colleagues who seem absolutely positive that they understand what is happening and know exactly what to do to rectify matters. I understand all too well how primitive the tools are that we therapists work with, how unreliable our methods, and how unpredictable the results. Show the same disabled vehicle to a half dozen mechanics, and there will be some degree of consensus among them as to what is wrong and what needs to be done. Yet show the same troubled person to a similar number of therapists, and there will likely be an assortment of different explanations of what is wrong and what should be done to fix it. What is truly amazing is that many of these professionals will be absolutely convinced that *their* diagnosis is accurate while the others are wrong, that *their* method of treatment is the only correct one. I know better.

As our field evolves, we are approaching greater rigor and consistency in our methods. For a certain number of complaints, say panic disorder, we even have reasonable agreement among many practitioners as to what should be done. Yet I have treated panic disorder clients successfully with many different methods. I have referred them for medication with good results. I have used behavior modification strategies, desensitizing them to their most fearful situations. That worked fabulously. I have employed hypnosis with dramatic effects. Even before I knew what I was *supposed* to do with such a case, I had worked successfully with clients by doing just what I usually do—creating a solid relationship in which it is safe to explore what the client's symptoms are really communicating. I suppose there were also times, probably more than I would prefer to admit, when I simply misdiagnosed the panic disorder as something else, say plain old anxiety, and plodded along with the treatment that worked best for that condition. The point is, however, that *all* of these treatments appear to work with some people some of the time, especially when employed by practitioners who believe in what they are doing.

Again, I am reminded of automobile mechanics. It is as if a particular mechanic has an extra supply of radiators, and so he really wants to believe that leaking fluids are responsible for all automobile breakdowns. He installs a new radiator on every car that limps in, regardless of what the trouble is. Amazingly, his strategy works!

I have known therapists who do only one thing, no matter who the client is and what is most distressing to him. Regardless of the presenting complaint, these therapists will only reflect feelings *or* interpret dreams *or* work on self-image exercises *or* structure behavioral goals *or* dispute irrational beliefs *or* explore families of origin *or* construct paradoxical directives *or* talk in metaphors. It is astounding to me that most of the time these professionals are indeed helpful!

There have been times in my career when I have used each one of these strategies and done so with the zeal of a true believer. Now I employ other methods, which directly contradict the assumptions of the previous ones. Does that mean that everything I have done before did not work after all? Was it all illusion?

Although filled with such doubts, I *did* begin to feel potent as a healer even while I was a skeptical student. When a new client entered my domain, I believed that I could offer some help. I may not have known exactly how long the helping process would take, nor would I have been altogether certain what I might have to do to effect desired results, but I had done the work for long enough to realize that practically everyone who agreed to work with me eventually got what they wanted. How could I exhibit such grandiose arrogance in the face of my previous confessions of skepticism? If I was getting good results, how was I deceiving myself? That is exactly what haunted me as a skeptical student, and it continues to bother me about my work to this day.

All the while I was sitting with a client, telling her with utter frankness that I thought—no, that I *knew*—what was bothering her, there was a voice inside my head that whispered, "You liar, Jeffrey. Who are you trying to kid? You don't have any more idea what this woman's problem is than you understand why big metal planes don't fall out of the sky or why big metal ships don't sink." This was assuredly true. Although I can talk about such phenomena in terms of displacement of air or water, they are nevertheless as magical to me as the process of therapy. I don't *know* how or why planes gorged with hundreds of tons of people, luggage, and fuel can lift off the ground much less stay aloft, but I am still willing to walk inside one and I do not worry much about getting to my destination.

As a skeptical student, I felt much the same way about therapy. I may not have understood too well what I did that worked so well, but I trusted the process as surely as I did the laws of physics. Long before Galileo, Newton, Einstein, Bohr, or Hawking discovered their underlying laws, these principles worked powerfully in our daily lives (although certainly, after they were identified, they could be harnessed more productively). Similarly, the real reasons why human change takes place and the laws governing how it takes place can remain buried yet still be potent. Nevertheless, I was bothered by not really understanding how therapy worked, nor knowing what I did that mattered most, just as I was haunted by the ghosts of those whom I could not help.

It was this feeling of impotence that propelled me out of the role of cynical student and into the position of vulnerable practitioner. I realized I would not find the answers in books or from my professors and supervisors. The paradoxes that bothered me so much did not seem to plague others whom I was around: "That won't be on the licensing exam," I was advised. "Just do your job and the rest will take care of itself."

In this way, I carried with me into my first professional sessions not only the remnants of my own unfinished business but also my skepticism about whether I was really doing anything with my clients. As long as things proceeded smoothly (which was rarely), I felt all right about this strange enterprise called therapy. More often, however, my doubts and uncertainties would flare up, especially when I encountered someone who did not improve. To this day, I am still haunted by the ghosts of those I could not help.

Part III

. . . .

Vulnerable Beginner

8

The Ones Who Got Away

Transitions from skeptical student to vulnerable practitioner, back to student again, and then once again out into the field had me feeling dizzy. During my master's degree program, one of my first jobs had been at a nursery school located on the grounds of an orphanage. I spent my days chasing three-year-olds while during the evenings I worked at a crisis center fielding phone calls from the desperate and lonely.

In both of my jobs, I felt immersed in mud, weighted down by the hopelessness of trying to help little and big people alike with very few resources. It seemed that the best thing I could do for the children was to hug them, to show them there was one male adult in the world whom they could count on. I tried to teach them how to share and be nice to one another, but having a dozen preschoolers within my sole charge was like standing guard over a room full of drunks. Since we were outside most of the time, their restless energy knew few bounds. I finally devised a method of organizing a race without a finish line, in which I would run them around and around in a big circle until they collapsed into exhaustion. Only then would they pay attention long enough to learn how to use a scissors or ruler.

During my evening job at the crisis center, I was dealing with even more severe problems. At least the children had a chance to grow up and make positive changes in their lives. The crisis callers were so strung out on drugs it seemed they just wanted to make contact with someone, anyone, before they continued their downward descent into hell.

I had originally hoped that getting a master's degree as a counselor would not only teach me the skills and knowledge I needed to help these people but would also make me feel validated and less vulnerable. Oh, I could talk with reasonable fluency about theories of career development or personality assessment. I could role-play with my peers *very* well, helping them to see the error of their ways in a matter of minutes. I could even establish rapport fairly well with the clients I worked with under supervision. But there was a whole additional universe of desperate people out there, wounded, suffering, disadvantaged, who would never enter the places where I would be waiting for clients. What could I do for them?

I reasoned that maybe if I had a doctorate I would feel more respectable and more prepared to be helpful. After all, everyone knows that Ph.D.'s are smart. If getting that first graduate degree hadn't worked as well as I had hoped in proving to myself that I was a competent human being (although I was feeling better about myself than before), perhaps having the title doctor in front of my name would give me instant respectability—in my own eyes if not my father's.

Once I had completed my doctorate, I did notice that I could get better restaurant reservations, but it then occurred to me that if that were my sole purpose I could have just awarded myself the title and saved a lot of aggravation. Nevertheless, with my limited experience as a practitioner and the exuberance of youth, I decided to hang out in the ivory towers of academe for a while longer.

Being a professor, a teacher of other therapists, seemed like a place where I might fit in. It struck me that being on campus I could have all the joys of a student but none of the difficulties. Since this time I would be the professor, I could do whatever I like. Besides, I would not have to take any more examinations; I could give them.

Surviving in Private Practice

After a brief stint in academic life at the only institution where I could find a job, I felt restless and stale, exiled not only to one of the most remote places in the South, but doomed to teaching students whose greatest point of pride was that their institution had produced the most winners of the Miss Alabama pageant. I had to escape from the isolation not only to preserve my sanity but also because I was itching to try being a full-time practitioner again. I also felt that I might be too young and inexperienced to be teaching other people to do what I only had limited experience doing.

Jobs were tight, however. I had received a grant that sent me to teach and consult in Peru for six months, but after that the only option I could find was to return back home with my wife and infant son to Michigan, where I might establish a private practice. It seemed like a good idea to simply start over again (but then that *always* seems like a good idea to me); however, our decision to leave Alabama was somewhat impulsive, and we had not thought through its implications. In fact, I was desperate. We had little savings. I could not have found a salaried position even if I had wanted one.

I thought that if I would hang out a shingle then clients would somehow appear at my door. After all, I was nice guy. I kind of knew what I was doing; at least I was a good pretender. Other people couldn't possibly know how vulnerable I felt. I distributed letters, made phone calls telling people I was around, printed up some business cards, and then waited for the public to find me. It didn't happen. After two months, I had three clients. Then one moved out of town. I was down to two. Bills were piling up and very little money was coming in. Finally, a new client showed up, referred by someone down the hall in the building where I had my office. I greeted her warmly (I hoped not too enthusiastically) and gave her some forms to fill out in the waiting room. I said I would return shortly.

I sat in my office staring at the clock, trying to figure out how long she would need to complete the paperwork. I calculated in my mind how many more clients like her I would need in order to survive at a minimal level. As bleak as times had been, it seemed this was an omen that they were looking better. For the first time in weeks, I felt real hope. But when I went back out to escort this new client inside, I discovered that my waiting room was now empty. Scribbled on top of the intake forms was a note that said she was sorry but she just couldn't go through with it. There went one-third of my prospective income. I was crushed.

I have been haunted by this woman, and many like her, ever since. Why did she leave? What did I do or say that drove her away? What might I have done differently? Could someone else have helped her in ways that I could not?

Whereas within a year income stopped being as much a consideration, I continued to feel a degree of desperation in getting clients to return. Many times I have heard myself say to students, "The object of a first interview is to get the client to come back for a second one. If the client will not return, you cannot help him." I have also advised beginners, over and over again, that therapists can not be all things to all people. No matter how good we are, no matter how skilled, experienced, and flexible, we can not reach everyone.

I must not believe what I say, however, because every time a client does not return I take it *very* personally. Against my better judgment, I feel rejected, just as I did in high school. If only I were better looking, more charming, or intelligent; if only I came from a better family or wore nicer clothes, then she would have liked me. Of course, I tell myself, this is ridiculous. Just because a client does not return does not mean I have failed or am somehow deficient. Maybe she already received enough help and does not need to return ("Yeah, right," I think). Perhaps I gave her enough to work on and she needs some time to digest it all ("Dream on"). Probably something completely unrelated to me intervened in such a way that she couldn't come back, even though she really wanted to ("Now you're really stretching things"). Then again, maybe she realized how powerful I am, and she just can't handle all that I have to offer ("Give me a break").

Is this a male thing, I wonder? What is it with me and rejection that I don't simply accept that I can't help everyone, no matter how hard I try? Why must I assume that a client's failure to return is evidence that I really am worthless? I have worked with at least a hundred clients who present this exact configuration of perfectionist demands. I have helped almost all of them, but I cannot seem to get through to myself.

Even worse for me than the clients who never return are the ones I have grown to care about and yet cannot seem to do much to help. I may have made a significant difference to many people, who left far better off than they were before, yet there are a dozen whose ghosts still haunt me. These are people who stayed with me for some time. They were in excruciating pain, and they looked to me for some hope. During the depths of their despair, I promised them that if they stuck with it long enough, if they really worked hard and made a commitment to their therapy, they would indeed see dramatic improvements. I was wrong.

I have every reason to know that a certain percentage of clients who seek help do not improve with any form of therapy. They may have some organically based disorder that is impervious to psychological intervention, or they may simply not be good candidates for what it is that we do. Something in their personalities or defense systems protects them to the extent that little can get through. When I read such arguments in the literature, I shake my head in solemn agreement. I know this. It is perfectly reasonable to assume that any given treatment will not prove helpful with everyone. However, I simply refuse to give up when that suffering person is within my care. Call it a god complex or just my inflated sense of power, but I really do believe that given enough time and patience, the client and I will work things out.

I remember their faces. I see their images on the walls as I hike through the narrows. I hear their voices crying out to me during the nights when I can't sleep. I feel them inside me, no matter how hard I work to shut them out.

One man came to me religiously for years. He wanted so badly to move away from his mother, to be able to get a job, to support himself, and I did everything I could think of to help him, all with little observable effect. I haven't seen this man in over a decade, but he still cries out to me when everything else inside me is still, "Please. Please help me. You've got to get me out of here!"

Then his plaintive wail is drowned out by another, much quieter voice. I hear the sniffles and sobs of a woman who would not talk to me much at all—she spoke in the language of tears. Her sense of hopelessness and despair was so profound I never had the chance to know her, much less help her. She killed herself after leaving my office.

Another man, whom I grew quite close to, seemed to enjoy our sessions a lot. We had fun together, and he seemed to be learning a lot too, making progress in the areas that were important to him. Imagine my surprise when one day he didn't show up for his appointment. He would not return my calls, nor would he pay his outstanding bill. Several months later, I received a request from another therapist in town to transfer his records to her. To this day, I have no idea what happened. I pretend to shrug indifferently, to think, "Oh well, you can't reach everyone." It still bothers the hell out of me.

I have not told many people how deeply I am affected by the ghosts of those I could not help. I am afraid of being seen as too weak for this sort of work. I should be able to let these images go, to move on to someone or something else. Does anyone realize how much is at stake for me with every client I see?

As a skeptical student, I doubted everything and everyone, myself most of all. Now as a beginning practitioner, I was almost as vulnerable. I did not yet believe in my own healing power. I could see some significant progress as a result of my labors, with myself as much as with my clients, but I wondered if the effects would last. My "customers" seemed satisfied, but what if they just *appeared* that way? What if they were only pretending to get better so they didn't hurt my feelings? What if at midnight the magic wore off, and like Cinderella, they regressed back to where they had been? What if . . . ?

Nagged by such doubts and consumed by feelings of powerlessness with those who needed my help, I found there never seemed to be enough that I could do for them. There was always more that I could have done. My very worth as a human being somehow seemed to get caught up in my competence *at any moment* as a professional. *That* is why there was so much at stake for me with everyone I tried to help. *That* is why I remained so vulnerable.

Too Much at Stake

Back when "St. Elsewhere," a popular television show about a hospital, was on the air, I once got into a discussion with some friends about which one of the doctors on the show we would choose for a personal physician and why. Most of my compatriots chose one of the stars, characters who loved to function under pressure and who were at the top of their class and brilliant in words as well as deeds.

I picked the perpetual dunce. He tried twice as hard as everyone else but always seemed to lag behind. I wanted him for my doctor because he took things so personally. If perchance I should die, I just knew that he would feel bad about it for the rest of his life. I liked those stakes; we would each have something precious to lose.

Maybe I live by the same stakes. The price I pay for helping some people is that I carry a part of the ones I can't help around inside me as a living legacy. If I could consciously let them go (and several of the images are fading over time, replaced by newer versions), I don't think I would wish to. There is no martyrdom in this that I am aware of. The bottom line for me is simply that my relationships with clients and students are very real to me. These people are as much a part of my life as my friends, my family, my colleagues, and my acquaintances.

I realize this is not a popular opinion in my field. In these days of "managed care," institutionalized, impersonal health programs, increased technology, and empirically based therapeutic interventions, relationships between human beings get lost in the shuffle. Beginning therapists are supposed to learn to build boundaries between themselves and those they help. It is good for clients to learn appropriate limits and good for therapists to insulate themselves from suffering. But no matter how long I stay in this line of work, I cannot seem to become completely desensitized to the misery I must encounter. I care too much. The client's life is not mine, yet in some ways he and I are resonating with one another's pain.

I guess I have never mastered the basic survival skill of marking boundaries. Perhaps that is why I move around so much: in the absence of self-imposed internal mechanisms to protect me from the onslaught of clients' pain and colleagues' political manipulations, I use geographical distance to start over again. If I were my own therapist (and of course I am), I might also suggest that if I met my needs for intimacy in other relationships in my life perhaps I would not be so vulnerable in relationships with my clients, students, and colleagues.

But I don't really buy that. I would fire myself as a therapist for misunderstanding myself if I truly suggested that interpretation. Of course, there is some truth to it—I do get my personal needs met in my work. I have evolved a style of practice that works quite well for me, and more importantly, for those I am trying to help. And however much I may be rationalizing why I care so much, why I am reluctant to let go of the high stakes I set up for myself, I also recognize that this caring is what impels me to try harder.

The fact is, I am simply not satisfied with mediocrity in what I do. I am not willing to repeat the same lectures over and over again or to make the same points with every client. I promise you, this is a heck of a commitment after twenty years of working in the same field. Yet I see this attitude as being at the heart of what makes me most powerful and most vulnerable.

I remember the ones who got away in order to remind myself how tenuous are my illusions of healing. When I do help someone, I don't play nearly as important a role as I would like to believe. When a client does not improve, or does not return, it is not as much a reflection of my failure as I pretend. And part of my growth from vulnerable beginner to confident veteran involved learning to harness my own pain, so that I could learn from those I couldn't help rather than pretend they did not exist.

9

Drawing on My Pain

A pediatrician once told me what was for him an old joke, when I asked him how he could stand listening to babies crying all the time. "Those aren't babies crying, he replied with a curdled smile, "that is the sound of cash registers ringing." Although I chuckled politely, I was appalled. I wouldn't let this guy near my kid, no matter how much he was hurting.

The sound of a baby crying produces about the most heart-wrenching, helpless feeling imaginable. After we have exhausted all the reasonable possibilities—he isn't wet, hungry, tired, choking, or cold—we are left to ponder what it might be that is causing such excruciating anguish. We might change his position, carry him around the room, distract him with strange sounds, block our own ears, but still the high-pitched screams sear us to the core: "Help me! Please help me! Why won't you do something!"

I will always remember the nights when I closed my son's door to block out his noise, hiding in the farthest corner of the house, finally walking him up and down the street in an endless procession, knowing that if I stopped for a moment his cries would begin anew. The pain of a helpless child continues to plague me because I must confront on a daily basis the torment of so many others who scream out for relief. Yet unlike the pediatrician, I do not hear their potential to add to my income as much as I feel the accusations, just as I did from my son, "Why don't you *do* something?"

Perhaps another major difference for me is that, compared to the pediatrician, I can offer so little. I wish I had some medication or procedure that would quickly remove a client's suffering. Heck, I would even settle for a definitive answer as to what the problem is. Instead, I must stay in the same room with the client's pain and try to offer some degree of comfort to the client: grieving parents who have lost their child to a degenerative disease; a woman so steeped in a depressive stupor she doesn't have enough energy to kill herself—it's too much trouble to jump, and with her luck, she believes she would survive the fall but be permanently crippled; an adolescent who is so lonely he cries himself to sleep each night, his last conscious thought the wish that he would not wake again; a man whose wife left him and who sees no reason to care about anything ever again; another man who lost custody of his children, and then his sanity.

As a vulnerable beginner, I saw an endless stream of pain file in and out of my office. There were people so anxious that they would not venture out of their safe little worlds, others hurting so badly they couldn't imagine a time in the future when things could be better, suffering a depression of such magnitude it was like a palpable cloud of pollution filling the room. Long after such people walked out, I was left to breathe the poisonous fumes that invaded my own soul.

Try as I might, I couldn't close out the pain. I might have *appeared* detached and objective, but inside I was crawling with despair. I *had* do something. I *had* to help these people. Unfortunately, I didn't know what to do for them any more than I knew how to stop my son's crying. It just seems that with many people the pain must run its course. I can offer words of encouragement. I can provide some company so the person does not feel so alone. Like waiting for the baby's exhaustion or boredom to set in, I brace myself and try to show patience and confidence. I want to close my ears, leave the room, change the channel. But I know I must stay until the end. And next Wednesday, at the same time, the vigil will continue, sometimes for months or years on end.

Harnessing Pain Therapeutically

There is some comfort in knowing that listening to others' pain is helpful to them. Not only do they feel accepted and understood, but miraculously, they complain less to their friends and relatives. It is as if the opportunity to dump their troubles for an hour a week means they don't need to dwell on their suffering as much at other times. I am the receptacle.

The problem of bearing others' pain is compounded because I carry my own pain as well. It is always with me, like a companion who sits just out of view. The dialogue I have with my client is thus accompanied by conversations within me, like this:

Client: It is as if no matter what I do, there is no sense in even trying. I will always be this way. Why should I even bother?

Me: Good question. *[And it is a good question. Sometimes I wonder the same thing.]* But you do have a choice. You don't have to stay in your present situation. You can get out. *[Yeah, sure. Then why don't I get out of this mess that I have created for myself? Why do I feel as helpless as she does?]*

Client: That's easy for you to say. You don't know what it feels like to be so stuck. I really want to quit my job but I just don't have the strength right now to deal with what would come afterwards. Someone like you probably couldn't relate to that.

Me: *[If she only knew.]* Look, I do know what that feels like. There have been times in my life when I have felt as stuck as you do now. I wanted to give up just like you do. *[What am I saying? I did give up several times. I remember . . . Oops. I've got to stay with her.]* Sometimes the pain simply becomes so intolerable that you no longer have a choice but to make the needed changes. It is no longer an option to remain in your present situation. *[I wonder if I am speaking to her, or to myself? So when am I going to take a stand and make the changes I need to initiate? I'm as afraid as she is of what is lurking around the corner.]*

Client: It is just so hard! (*Sobs.*) I just . . . (*Several minutes go by while silent tears stream down her face. Finally she looks up expectantly, waiting for me to do something.*)

But I don't know what to do. I feel as helpless as she does. Her pain and mine are intermingled. I am trying to separate which part of what is going on belongs to her and which part is mine. Yet because I understand so well what she is experiencing, I do know what to do now. I know what I wanted someone to say to me, what I needed in order to break loose from the bonds of feeling helpless. I try that with her, and she feels understood by me at the very least. Quite possibly, I have reached her in a way that will allow her to experiment with taking some risks.

If I try to distract myself from the anguish of clients' lives, I have no place to retreat except my own castle of despair. I look out from the watchtower, surrounded by enemies on all sides. Over there, right out in the open, is an army composed of those whom I could not help. They limp along, crying piteously, firing accusations of incompetence and inadequacy with deadly accuracy. There, lurking along the lip of the forest, is an ambush waiting to happen should I be so foolish as to venture forth on a crusade. The infidels in this fiendish band have done their homework. They know just which route I am likely to take, just as surely as they know the bait that will hook me again. These are the people in my life, past and present, whom I still allow to control me.

Where was I? Oh, yes. I was concentrating on my client's pain. How easily I lapse into my own, forgetting that I am supposed to be keeping watch in someone else's castle. I have a hard time keeping our dwellings separate. Everything the client says triggers something in me. As long as I am listening, I relate to this person as an observer *and* a participant.

I grew as a therapist by learning my own pain was my greatest resource. It wasn't my knowledge or skills alone that made a difference; it was the stark clarity with which I could feel the pain of others and connect it to my core issues. My clients found in me not only a confidante but a compatriot, a partner in pain. I could inspire them because I knew their experiences, just as they could feel my vulnerability.

When someone would tell me about feeling so lonely that her chest hurt, I would nod my head in remembrance of a similar experience. When another would tell me about feeling that his life was a failure, I would interrupt and tell him what he could not put into words. He would look at me in wonderment: "How did you know that?" I was convincing because what he was saying was real for me as well. Yet I was also someone who had overcome my adversity. I appeared powerful and in control. I was a living example to them that therapy works in the sense that it is possible to move beyond pain, to use its lessons to appreciate the pleasure of daily existence. I had taught myself to move beyond my pain, to live with it as a friend, to embrace its teachings.

This is not the confession of a masochist. I *hate* suffering. I am positively allergic to it. I am not willing to devote a single hour of my life to feeling anxious or depressed. When I catch myself in self-pity, I throttle myself, therapeutically speaking, until I am clear-headed once again. My favorite food is a jalapeño pepper or anything equally spicy. Objectively, the sensation of biting into a pepper is physically painful; it literally hurts. Yet it is a pain that opens up the pores, floods me with sensation, stimulates my brain, wakes me up to notice how good it feels to be alive. I think of my emotional pain in the same way. I am no longer ashamed of my vulnerability; I now know that I cannot be hurt as long as I stay focused on what it has to teach me.

When that focus doesn't work, I also know how to escape the pain, if not mute its intensity, just as with practice we come to perfectly control a water spigot, turning it on or off or adjusting pressure and temperature. Our transitions from vulnerable beginners to accomplished veterans is often a matter of what we do on the inside, how we think and process what is going on, rather than what we do or say aloud.

A Catalogue of Pain

During my early years of practice, I felt strongly ambivalent about the people I tried to help. I resonated with their misery and yet despised them for being victims. They reminded me how tenuous were my own illusions of control.

One client reminded me of an alien from another planet. We were about as different as two people can be. "Marjorie" lived on the streets while I was a super-responsible suburban yuppie. She wondered where her next meal would come from while I thought about which fine restaurant I would go to for dinner. She wondered where she would find a new coat that would be warm enough to get her through the winter; I was undecided whether I should go to the beach or ski slopes during my vacation.

With good reason, Marjorie mistrusted me immensely. Why did I care what happened to her? Was this just a job for me? Was I just trying to earn points to get into heaven? Was I thinking about what a good story she would make? She looked me up and down with the identical disdain that I resisted showing as I surreptitiously examined her. When was the last time she had had a bath? Could that hair color possibly be real? What does she carry in that bag? We sized one another up with the crushing disappointment of the parties to a futile blind date.

She all but told me I was worthless to her. She began a litany of complaints so comprehensive, so utterly tragic and encompassing, that I wondered how she could even stand under the weight of so much disappointment and disaster. Her pain reached out to me. It was so hot, I couldn't even touch it. I backed away—feeling burnt just from being in close proximity. She felt my rejection, or at least distancing, and withdrew back into her broken body. I struggled with wanting to be as far away from her as I could, yet feeling how we were both growing when we stayed close.

In that same instant, I could feel her pain at a temperature that was manageable for me. Or was it *my* pain now? I have flashbacks to times in my life when I felt like a leper—how easy it is for me to imagine that everyone else is better than me, more worthy. I think that it is pure luck that landed us in our respective positions. I could easily be in her ill-fitting shoes. What does it feel like to give up so completely, I ask myself, but the thought is so frightening that I turn that faucet off. Marjorie sees me visibly shaking. She seems to realize this is not in response to her, that I have my own demons. When I open myself up to her, say something about knowing what her pain must feel like, she realizes she is no longer alone. I have been convincing because I really do feel my pain as a companion to hers. This is no act.

I have a catalogue of pain that I can draw from at will. Each page has full-color pictures, complete with prices and descriptions. If I turn to the section "Incidents from Childhood," I find myself once again sitting alone in my room, huddled in a corner, rocking back and forth, wondering how I will survive now that my father has left and I must now take care of my mother and brothers.

I flip to "Adolescence in Action." There I am again in my room, a different room but a dungeon nevertheless, playing the guitar this time, blocking out all other sounds. Between the guitar and masturbation, I could block out the pain of loneliness for hours on end, interchanging one instrument for another, anesthetizing myself. I felt so alone that even my tears cried out in anguish.

Fast forward to college now. I am running through a field, running as hard as I can, until I cannot run any more. I fall exhausted to the ground. I roll over, stare at the sky, and think about the best way to kill myself. I decide pills would be the best, but where do I get them and how many should I take? Nah, better just to ram my car into a tree. Much simpler and more certain. Maybe I could find a gun somewhere. . . . A bird lands on a fence post near where I lie plotting my death. He stares down at me and asks what the problem is. I am so lost that I begin talking to this bird, trying to explain to him why I cannot go on anymore. The bird shakes his head and flies away. Now I am truly alone.

The catalogue flips over a few more pages. I somehow survive into my twenties, channeling my pain into compulsive achievement and study. My mother is dying of cancer; my father is having a coronary bypass. A late bloomer and slow learner in the counterculture of the sixties, I finally discover drugs. I begin with marijuana, and then move on to experimenting with cocaine, LSD, downers, uppers—all in trial doses. Fortunately, I am blessed with a nervous system that finds these substances amusing yet is not so entranced that I feel a compulsion to abuse them. But why was I so stubborn about not trying these substances earlier in life? Did I so enjoy the attention and novelty of being the only one at parties who could remember what happened the next day? Whatever my reasons, they no longer seem to matter. Drugs work even better than music and masturbation to keep the pain under control. But not as well as therapy.

Life as a Client

When someone asks my advice about the best way to learn to be a therapist, which degree or program is most advantageous, which books are most instructive, who are the best mentors in the field, I always recommend that they first see a good therapist.

"Excuse me," I hear in return, "perhaps you didn't understand me. I don't need a referral to a therapist; I want to *be* a therapist." Same thing, I tell them. Most of what I mastered as a practitioner, I learned the hard way, sitting in the client's chair. My first such experience was as a college student when I was spinning out of control over a lost love. I believed myself to be stone crazy, on my way to a life in mental hospitals. The therapist I spent two years with was a psychoanalyst, which means she listened a lot while I talked. In the hundred or so sessions we spent together, she never talked for more than sixty minutes. In total. Yet it felt so good to have an attentive listener. I loved blurting out all my secrets to see if I could shock her but found that she could keep her face so still she must have also played poker.

She helped me, this mute woman who demanded nothing. I reveled in the freedom I felt when I found I could do almost nothing to alienate her. I was used to the women in my life being withholding, so her silence didn't bother me too much. Yet she seemed wise and omnipotent. She reassured me that I wasn't crazy, and I believed her. She finished the job that my mother couldn't complete. She was also dependable, and that I needed most of all at the time, someone who I knew would be there for me, even if being there was simply listening to me speak.

When I was in my master's program a few years later, one of my brothers had a toxic psychotic reaction to drugs and was hospitalized. I wrote about my despair in a paper for one of my classes, an open invitation for my professor to reach out to me. He responded by inviting me to join a therapy group he was leading, and I remained with the group throughout the rest of my program. It was here that I learned a great deal of what I now know about helping people. I loved this environment so much, I decided to make group work my specialty. I couldn't believe how wonderful it felt to belong, to feel the support of the other members. I loved confronting people and having them respond honestly in return. I got to try out some of the new skills I had been learning as well as note what worked with me.

During the next year, I grew at a pace that made me feel dizzy. I ended an engagement with a woman who was not good for me nor I for her. In the span of a few months, I quit a job working for my father's company to take the two part-time positions at the preschool and crisis center. I moved out of the suburbs into the inner city. My transformation was so complete that I emerged at the end of this group such a profoundly different human being that some of my friends no longer recognized me.

During the next decade, I probably needed to get back into therapy at various times, but I resisted for the same reason that most people do, thinking that I should be able to handle things myself. It was only after I felt completely lost and hopeless, burned out as a practitioner, and doomed to spend eternity living an empty life that I asked for help once again.

By this time, just as I had lost faith in myself, I had stopped believing in the healing powers of therapy. I couldn't trust just any one clinician, so I made appointments with three of them! I figured I would interview each of them, let them do their best stuff, and then choose the one I believed could help me the most. I found a lovely match with an older man who was my embodiment of a perfect father. He was accepting and loving but also a straight talker. I hated therapists who played "shrink games," acting in some professional role that I recognized all too well. I needed someone who would be real and genuine with me and who would talk to me in an open and honest way, inviting me to do the same.

My gosh, how I love being a client in therapy! It is even more fun than being in the other chair. Oh, to feel free to say whatever I want without fear of judgment or criticism! I love the permission to go deeper, to explore the further reaches of what is in my heart and soul. I love/hate it when a therapist says to me, "Okay, Jeffrey, now what is the *real* reason you are doing that?" or, "That's a load of bull! What are you going to do about that?"

I believe with all my heart that talking to other people, making intimate contact, is the best part of what I do. I am a good therapist because I was a good client. All the while I have learned to keep my pain under control, to harness its power in order to infuse my creativity and productivity, I have never forgotten the magic of feeling understood.

I notice that Marjorie seems transformed. She smells wonderful. I like the color of her hair. I can't wait to see her next time. I know that each meeting reopens some of my own wounds, but it is a good hurt, the kind that itches when it is healing.

Part IV

· ·

Compulsive Father

Compulsive Father, Inadequate Son

A relatively small part of growing into a therapist involves professional training. When you consider how much time we therapists spent as "civilians" long before we ever entered graduate school, you can appreciate that much of what we know comes from personal experiences in our own families, both our families of origin and those in which we presently reside. If my vulnerability as a beginning therapist emanated from events that transpired in my past, from relationships with the significant people who populated my childhood, then my growth and healing have been facilitated by my family in the present.

When I was a child, my father was the center of my universe, the stable parent figure with whom I over-identified, in spite of his absences. I tried to be the son that he wanted me to be, but I came up short in every category that mattered. I was a dismal failure as a student, which could be forgiven. On top of that, however, I could not play golf or tennis, nor was I willing to set foot at the country club where he was the star.

I never doubted for a moment that both my parents loved and accepted me dearly, foibles, mediocrity, and all. It was not so much that I felt disapproved of by them as I felt that I was letting them down. I was neither as smart as they were, as polished and easygoing, nor as talented. I'm not certain if I lived up to expectations of me that were low in the first place, or whether the low expectations followed from my poor performance at school, athletics, and the country club. In either case, in some ways I enjoyed a free ride as a kid. I could get away with certain behavior because my parents did not believe I was capable of doing much better.

With my parents living in their own worlds, my two brothers and I were pretty much left in the care of our housekeeper. She became my surrogate mother and father. However, probably more than anyone else, my grandfather was the person I looked to for support. He was the one other person who was there for me, no questions asked. He could not have cared less what I did with my life. He asked nothing of me except that I not fight with my brothers so much.

Every Saturday of my childhood, he picked my brothers and me up for an afternoon at the movies—four cartoons and two feature films. If we really liked a movie, sometimes he would even let us see it twice. He took me to see *The Time Machine* three times, then *The Alamo* a half dozen times over the next few months. I couldn't believe that anyone could be so endlessly patient, so giving of himself to others. He was my hero, and still is today. He was the perfect model of a loving human being who derived intense satisfaction from bringing pleasure to others. I could spend the rest of my life trying to duplicate his selfless giving and never pay him back.

Yet it was not only my grandfather's model that instilled in me a commitment to the service of others. As a young adult and new professional, I was still incredibly self-centered, measuring all that I did in terms of how it furthered my career or bank account. It was when my son was born, named after my grandfather, that I really learned what it meant to give of myself.

From Son to Father

I was not at all enamored with the idea of having a child. My wife, Ellen, and I had been getting along marvelously, and if there was a time in our twenty-year marriage when the relationship seemed precarious, it was during the first two years of parenthood. The sleepless nights, the lack of sex or intimacy, the financial pressures, the single-minded devotion to taking care of this needy being took their toll.

The same doubts I had about my ability to be a fine therapist were also part of my worries as a father. I desperately wanted to be a different sort of parent than my own father had been to me. For one thing, I wanted to know my son, to spend time with him on a daily basis. I also hoped that I could be accepting of who he was as a unique person, that I would not need him to fit into the mold that I preferred.

It is probably not surprising to you that it was not enough for me to be a good father or even a great one; I had to be a *perfect* parent. I will never forget the first time I yelled at my child, the first time I raised my voice in anger. We had been playing in the sandbox together, and while I was otherwise occupied, he dumped a bucket of sand over my head and started giggling. Before I could even think, I screamed at him to stop. He looked at me completely startled and broke out into a stream of tears. I had made him cry.

I know this sounds incredible, but until the last few years, when he hit adolescence, I could easily count the few times I had ever yelled at my son. *That* is how hard I have worked to be the perfect father. Does this mean that as a result of my compulsive labors my wife and I have turned out the ideal offspring? Hardly, and that *is* surprising, considering that my wife is even more patient than I am, more easygoing, and more devoted to our son's care.

It has taken many years for my son and me to grow up together. I have learned to be more forgiving of myself, and I am hopeful that he can follow my lead. So far, I would have to say this strategy has not been working, since he seems to be more driven than I am to succeed. He is surely less accepting of his own mistakes and failures, but I suspect (hope) that trait is age related.

Payback Time

As my son reaches into adulthood, it's payback time. I relive my childhood and now know what my father must have been going though while trying to make sense of my outbursts and tantrums.

As I entered adulthood, I recall feeling so relieved that finally the worst was over. Little did I realize that having a child would elicit in me the same feelings that had plagued my own childhood. When my son has nobody to play with, it's as if I am reliving my own inadequacies all over again. When a teacher is mad at him, it feels as if I am the one who messed up. Most disorienting of all, when I have been impatient with him or hurt him in some other way, I *simultaneously* feel like a father, and reliving a similar experience from my own childhood, like a hurt child.

My struggle and growth as a therapist has paralleled my evolution as a father. In both roles, I started out insecure and ill prepared to handle the critical incidents that come up on a daily basis. What do I say to my son who is obviously lying about some trouble he has found himself in? How do I get him to tell me about what he really feels inside when his best friend won't speak to him anymore? How do I talk to him about sex when he says he already knows it all? I am a therapist. I do this stuff for other people's children all the time. Why can't I figure out how to reach my own son any better than my father could connect to me?

In an effort to track my growth as a parent and therapist, I took to writing in a journal. It was in this safe place that I would talk to all the clients who left before I could say goodbye. It was also a place that I could speak to my son, to tell him the things that he wouldn't listen to in person. On the occasion of my son's eighth birthday, for instance, I wrote him the following letter which I have not shown him until this moment (he is now thirteen):

Dear Cary,

I was thinking about you a lot this morning. When I drove you to school, you were bouncing off walls you were so incredibly happy to be alive. I just kept seeing that toothless smile of yours, that muscular, vibrant body. I just want to tell you how much respect I have for you as a human being. Yes, at 8 years of age! I am writing this down because I am not sure you would understand what I mean, and even if you did, you get embarrassed about these things.

What I want to tell you is this: It is amazing to me what you have turned yourself into as a person. You are absolutely brilliant—a fearless truth seeker—inquisitive, your mind staggers me—what you know, what you remember, what you understand. You are aggressive as hell—you know no fear— you will take on anyone twice your size. Best of all, and what I am most proud of, you are such a nice person—kind, gentle, sensitive, and loving. You love to hug and be hugged. And gosh, I feel wistful and sad thinking about you growing up, leaving my lap. I dread the day when you will resent me terribly, when you will need to be your own person and so put me in my place by taking me on, as I did my own father.

I sit in my office all day and listen to people purge their anger and resentment about parents they felt were neglectful or abusive (as I also felt about my own). It saddens me to think that some day you will resent me too, that you will feel the need to distance yourself from me in order to find your own voice.

With much love,

Daddy

Writing such letters in my journal has helped me to clarify why being a compulsive father is not enough; parenting, like therapy, is not simply a matter of doing all the right things. Growing as a father, and as a professional helper, means being patient, like my grandfather. As much as I would like to believe that I can act perfectly competently through sheer force of will, I have come to recognize that the best I can do is to be with my son or my clients, to give them my love and compassion, and to leave the rest to them.

The Questions Never End

Among the most difficult challenges for a parent or a therapist are the questions that inevitably arise for which we have few answers. Clients often ask things that, though reasonable, are out of my grasp: (1) "How long will this therapy take?" (2) "How does this whole thing work, anyway?" (3) "So, what *is* my real problem?" (4) "What do *you* think the meaning of life is all about?"

As I have grown as a therapist, I have certainly learned to field these questions with skill if not real evasive artistry: (1) "How long therapy takes depends on you." (2) "Therapy works in a number of different ways; the best way to understand it is to experience it." (3) "What do *you* see is your real problem?" (4) "What I think is the meaning of life is less important than what you think. It is my job to help you answer that question to your own satisfaction."

With all this training and practice in fielding difficult questions, you would have thought I was well prepared to deal with the same challenges as a parent. I wasn't. One Sunday morning, I decided to write down a list of all the questions my son, then age seven, asked me in a single hour:

"How come when the catcher throws the ball back to the pitcher, I've never, ever seen him drop the ball?"

"If we were walking slow, and an ant was walking its fastest, would we still be faster because ants have smaller feet?"

"Daddy, what are you writing?"

"Doesn't an *E* in sign language look like a monster?"

"How long would it take to go across Walloon Lake sideways?"

"Can we play Yahtzee?"

"Why do the miles when we are on vacation seem so short compared to driving a mile when we are home?"

"When you're eighteen, how do you not go in the Army?"

"Daddy, why didn't you go in the war?"

"Will I have to go?"

"If you shot a bullet up in the air, would it go into space?"

"When are we leaving?"

Answering my son's questions has always been another way that I relive my own childhood. The difference is that this time I am doing things better. As I learn to be more accepting of my flaws as a parent, I become more accepting of the limitations of my own parents. In order for me to deal with my vulnerabilities, I must be willing to come to terms with my past. Being a parent gives me a chance to do that.

I don't mean that the success of my efforts depends on how well my child turns out, on what he does with his life. I am referring instead to the experience that I have, that all parents have when we live vicariously through our children. My son does not have to be what I want him to be or do what I wish him to do. Rather, I am following *his* lead. As he completes each year of his life, I am reliving that year in my own life. Vividly. In so doing, I can feel myself becoming more accepting of what took place in my life. My son has taught me that.

Coming to terms with my own past through my role as a parent has been the basis for much of the progress I have made as an adult. In my professional roles as colleague, teacher, therapist, and writer, I have been most effective when I can harness these experiences in such a way that I heighten my sensitivity to others.

A portion of my growth as a person, as well as a therapist, has resulted from my attempts to be less compulsive as a father and more adequate as a son.

Not So Alone After All

Therapists are supposed to be relationship specialists. We create intimacy for a living. We help people to trust us to the point where they will tell us their deepest secrets and reveal their innermost thoughts. I am at a loss to explain, therefore, how it is possible for some of us who are supposed experts at developing relationships in our professional capacities, to be so good at getting close to others when they are in our offices, but so unwilling to do so in our personal lives with partners, families, friends, and co-workers. Some therapists may see certain clients for years, engaging in the closest human encounters that are possible, and yet they can not or will not become very open in their civilian lives.

Try to get close to a therapist who wishes to keep you at a distance, and you will witness an impressive show of force.

"I see that you are interested in what I have to say."

"What is it like for you not being able to get me to respond the way you prefer?"

"You seem frustrated because I am not meeting your expectations."

"Perhaps you are not so much asking about me as you are saying something about yourself. I wonder what that might be?"

And when all else fails, there is this retort: "It is not so much that you want to get close to me as that you want to get close to someone else from your past whom I remind you of."

In other words, if a therapist wants to keep you from getting too close, it's not a problem. We have an unfair advantage in our relationships. We are used to being in control. We participate in intimate relationships all day long, in which people share their deepest selves, and yet we do not have to reciprocate. We get to be close to others without being hurt.

If that is not a major theme for others in my field, it certainly is for me. I had a hard time with relationships when I was younger. In high school, most of the girls I liked said they only wanted to be my "friend," not my "girlfriend," a distinction that escaped me. The only difference I could figure out was that a girlfriend you kissed on the lips and a girl who was a friend you kissed on the cheek. My raging hormones were not able to appreciate the subtleties of this distinction.

In college, relationships became a little easier for me. Mostly, this was because I wanted a girlfriend so badly it almost killed me. Literally. There was one relationship, in particular, in which I completely lost control of myself, lost the sense of who I was, even lost the ability to distinguish between fantasy and reality. There was a young woman who sat in front of me in a philosophy class. She was a goddess, completely out of reach. Yet something possessed me to approach her, and much to my surprise, we became infatuated with one another in a matter of hours.

Perhaps any relationship would be doomed that began at such a torrid pace. It lasted only a month, from beginning to end. The details are hazy for me and not because of the passage of time. Immediately after the relationship ended, I could not put the pieces together to figure out what happened to me. I think (or would like to believe) that I was physically ill in some way. I know that my temperature was elevated and my judgment was cloudy.

I had become so attached to this woman, so infatuated with her, so obsessed with our relationship that I wanted to possess her completely. I fantasized that when she was not with me, she was meeting someone else. Then when I saw her, I could not tell what had really happened and what was part of my imagination. Needless to say, this frightened the hell out of her. She dropped me off at the campus psychological services (where I met the psychoanalyst I mentioned earlier), and that was the last I saw of her.

It took months, if not years, for me to recover from this experience. I was despondent, if not downright suicidal. My worse nightmare had been realized: this event proved I really was crazy. I had lost control of myself. I had let myself care so much for somebody else that I could not function. I vowed this would never happen again. Furthermore, I set out to equip myself with whatever it took to make me invulnerable.

Learning to be a therapist, first as a client and later as a practitioner, did not disappoint me in this regard. I did find that I had the means to protect myself better. And I built myself up so I was strong enough to risk loving again, albeit in a different way. You see, I believed that love was overrated, at least the romantic, infatuated kind that we see in the movies. I had had a taste of that now and had not found it altogether agreeable.

A Life Partner

I have been married now for twenty years to the same person, a circumstance that I find improbable after the inauspicious way our marriage began. I vividly remember walking down the aisle, music welling up in the background, our fate linked by this ceremony witnessed by our friends and relatives. I recall thinking to myself at the time, not how excited I was about our future, but about how dishonest I felt about repeating the vows that were waiting at the end of this ceremony. I could not in my wildest imagination believe that it would be possible for me to stay in a relationship with the same woman for years, much less decades, even one whom I believed I loved.

As I continued the cadenced stroll, trussed up just like a soldier in my marital uniform, I caught out of the corner of my eye a most attractive young woman sitting on my future wife's side of the aisle. Who is this person, I wondered, at the exact moment she flirtatiously winked at me. I thought then that I was making a terrible mistake.

Two decades have elapsed since that day, and however amazed I am by our staying power, we are still married. While I often wonder how we have managed to remain together, given our basic differences and incompatibilities, there is no doubt in my mind that support from my wife, and later my son, has been the foundation for my emotional stability. They have taught me how to love, slowly, carefully—not in leaps and bounds but in those same small, cautious steps with which I walk through the narrows during the most challenging stretches.

Through deaths, crises of faith and hope, personal doubts, betrayals by those I have trusted, and excursions through my dark side, my family has helped me to flourish. I can now love without fear of rejection, without feeling so vulnerable that I might be destroyed in the process. I have grown as a therapist so that I can capture my compassion and caring to be a healing force with my clients. I am much more impressed, however, with how I have learned to be more loving with my friends and family.

This has not been easy for me. I am a selfish son of a bitch. I am impulsive and self-centered. I am irresponsible when it comes to managing money or making mature, adult decisions. I first figure out what I want to do and how I am going to make it happen; then I worry about the consequences. I am a hedonist, an unrelenting pursuer of pleasure. And while obeying my primary moral imperative to do no harm to others, I am an insatiably curious sensation seeker.

My wife, on the other hand, is the embodiment of traditional values—stable, predictable, conventional, socially appropriate, scrupulously responsible, completely giving of herself. We balance one another: I bring out her more adventurous side while she tem-

pers my spontaneous urges to go full speed ahead without considering what may be waiting around the next corner.

I am game to go anywhere, do most anything. As content as I
am with where we live and what we are doing, I would drop it all
and move elsewhere at the drop of pin or, more to the point, the
ringing of the phone. In fact, such a call came this very week, an
invitation to take up a challenge in another part of the world. I
immediately begin thinking about how I could make this happen,
how exciting it would be to start over again. It is my wife who asks
the hard question of me: What is it that I am looking for that I don't
already have?

I love this woman dearly, respect her as I have no other person
on earth. We get along as smoothly as two perfect friends can. We
hardly ever argue. I can barely recall a time when we have ever raised
our voices to one another in anger. When we are upset with one
another, Ellen cries; I withdraw and pout. We are mutually supportive of one another and have done our best to function as a team. We
are, thus, fabulous parents; I cannot imagine any who are better.

After twenty years together, we often live together more as
roommates rather than lovers. Like so many couples who stay
together out of habit, we take each other for granted. We have
heard each other's stories a hundred times. We are so preoccupied
with the many details of daily life—working our jobs, taking care of
our home, driving our son to baseball practices, attending social
functions—that we rarely relate to one another romantically. By
the time we see one another at the end of a long, hectic day, we are
often too tired to listen to one another, much less take the time to
relate in an intimate way. Sex has become an occasional event that
occurs during those rare times when both of us are awake and not
otherwise occupied.

We are the mold of the modern couple. I know this from all the
years I have been doing marital counseling. We get along fabulously;
no major problems. I wonder, though, where all the passion has
gone. Is this what happens with maturity? We become comfortable

with one another? Every few years, we attempt to stir things up, and things feel renewed for a little while, but like any being or process that is living, without considerable nurturance, a relationship will become stagnant. Ours is no exception.

Oasis of Support

A sense of family is an oasis of support in a lonely desert yet also tremendous heartache. I recall when my son was born, the incredible fear and vulnerability I felt that forever after I would be terrified that something I love more than my own life could somehow be harmed. I see my son, no, I *feel* him hurting because a friend does not return his call or a girl he likes doesn't like him back. He drops a line drive or misses an easy lay up, and it is *I* who feel the humiliation. Every time he is up at the plate to bat, my heart pounds so hard that my ribs hurt from the ricochets. Each of his disappointments feels like my setback, and I certainly already have enough of my own.

I just never imagined that one of the consequences of having a kid was that I would have to relive my own painful childhood. I was reasonably prepared for the sleepless nights and stress on my marriage. I had even been sufficiently warned about the challenges that come with adolescence. I had no idea, however, of the extent to which I would become enmeshed in his life, sometimes unable to separate where he ends and I begin. I know that these troubles are just beginning as he now enters the full blossom of his adolescence.

I am supposedly an expert on these situations. I advise parents how to handle their children. I tackle rebellious teenagers that other professionals have long abandoned. I write books for teachers, counselors, and therapists about how to handle difficult, resistant adolescents. I do workshops for other experts on how to work through impasses with noncooperative children. Yet I remember the day I was sitting in my office at home, holding a supervision session with another therapist who was having difficulty with a resistant family. She was feeling grateful for my wise counsel and my innovative suggestions as to how she might break through the resistance. I was feeling powerful and helpful in my efforts, thinking that I *am* an adolescent at heart, never having outgrown my own impulsiveness and exuberance. I speak their language and can read their minds, so naturally I can reach them wherever they might hide. It was at this very moment of self-congratulation that I glanced out the window and noticed my son riding up the driveway on his bike. My son? What was *he* doing home? He was supposed to be in school.

I abruptly ended the supervision session and sent the therapist on her way, so that I could deal with this unusual situation. Tears were streaming down Cary's face; he could not talk through the sobs. One message was very clear: he was not willing to go back to school. Not now. Not ever. I attempted to reason with him, to listen compassionately and offer support. When that failed, I felt utterly helpless: "Look, you have to go to school. You don't have a choice. Come on, I'll take you back." He would have no part of any reasoning, any argument, any threat. Quite simply, he did not feel safe at school. He was scared something bad would happen, and this fear for his personal safety seemed to override anything I could do to convince him to go.

Not five minutes earlier, I had been feeling and acting the part of adolescent expert. I knew just what to do with other people's kids. So why couldn't I figure out what to do with my own? Cary and I talked for a while. Eventually, we agreed to meet with his counselor and figure out some course of action. Since it was the one-year anniversary of his best friend's having been shot at school during an argument with another kid, it was perfectly understandable that he would be experiencing some posttraumatic symptoms. Apparently, other children were showing signs as well.

We worked out the problem, and in a matter of days, all returned to normal. Yet such challenges are occurring with greater frequency in our home, and as every parent well knows, there is nothing more excruciating for a human being to live through, nothing more upsetting for marital partners to come to terms with. This is the price we pay for caring so deeply for others.

These are the two people whom I am closest to, whom I trust with my life. We are comfortable with one another, accustomed to one another's rhythms. Yet sometimes, I feel stifled by my wife and son. I feel them draining my energy and resources. I wonder if I have sold out by settling for conventionality instead of carving out another version of my life that could be more to my liking. I have gone along with the flow, done what has been expected, because it was easier.

I have no idea if I will still be married to the same person in another twenty years, or twenty days for that matter. However hopeful I might be, I don't know if I will still be on speaking terms with my son as he continues his journey toward adulthood. There was a time when I couldn't imagine spending a whole night away from home without missing him so much I couldn't sleep or function. Even now, the prospect that he will some day move out of the house paralyzes me with dread. I see my own father about once a year, and he does not really know me. Will my own relationship with my son come to that? I cannot think about that possibility without feeling a searing pain knife through me. Although I know, rationally and intellectually, that by the time that might happen I will be as ready as anyone could be to handle the situation (after all, I have already lived through it a few dozen times with my clients), I am still filled with anticipatory dread.

Yet with all the aggravation and challenges that are part of getting along with those I live with, I do not feel alone now that I am part of this family. If I as a parent must relive my childhood, let me do so in the company of those I trust to hold my hand in the dark. If I am to come to terms with my imperfections as a husband, a father, and a therapist, I must do so with the support of people I love and with whom I can risk being vulnerable.

That, after all, is what I ask of my clients and students. I urge them to trust me. I try to care enough about them that maybe they will care more for themselves. I work to accept them, even if I have such trouble accepting my own parts that are less than perfect. As I get closer to feeling comfortable in my own skin, so too do I feel more satisfied with the supportive relationships in my life.

Part V

. . . .

Imperfect Therapist

12

Obsessed with Failure

I have had the misfortune to work around a number of wounded healers. For a while, I wondered if anyone in my field had his or her act together, so pervasive seemed to be the dysfunctions of my colleagues. However, this discovery did not bother me nearly as much as I would have thought, mostly because I was obsessed with my own sense of failure.

No matter how much I read and studied, how many workshops I attended, how much supervision I participated in, how many degrees I obtained, or how much experience I gained, I could never learn enough. I was preoccupied with the mistakes I made in every session, the things I could have said or done better. I was haunted by those I could not help. Even the clients who were making progress did not provide much comfort: if I were smarter or more talented, I could have helped them faster.

A trusted colleague once confided to me her own fears of failure. She had been struggling to come to terms with the recent suicide of a client; as impaired and inadequate as she felt, she was now questioning whether it was safe for her to continue practicing. From this conversation, others ensued on the same subject, and we eventually decided to collaborate on a research project in which we would interview other clinicians about their experiences with failure. There was quite a personal motive involved in this endeavor: maybe we would feel better about ourselves if only we knew that others felt the same way, that they were as unforgiving, as unable to disown their failures as we secretly were.

You see, this is a subject we therapists almost never speak about, not even to ourselves. It is as if our admission that we are somehow less than omnipotent and flawless will cost us our power to heal. Our most closely guarded secret is that most of the time we don't really know what we are doing; we are faking it, buying time until we can figure out what is going on. We certainly don't draw attention to our mistakes, nor do we acknowledge our misjudgments. In our staff meetings, we rarely talk about those cases in which we need the most help; we are overly concerned with looking good in front of our peers. This behavior was modeled for us during our training years by professors who rarely talked about cases in which they had failed, just as our texts always presented perfect examples of how things were supposed to work. Nobody told us that clients don't always follow the rules. Nobody mentioned that most of the time we would be stumbling around in the dark.

I don't wish to imply that members of our profession are not highly skilled diagnosticians and experts but inept and incompetent. That is not the case. But like lawyers, physicians, and almost every other professional, we are paid to act as if we know what we are doing all of the time. "I don't know," "I made a mistake," and "I'm sorry" are completely unacceptable statements. If you doubt this, once again imagine how you would feel if you heard a therapist tell you the truth: "How should I know what your problem is? I just met you. I'm not even sure I can help you, or when I will know the answer to that, or how long this will take."

No wonder I am obsessed with failure. I will never know enough. I will always be imperfect.

From Academician to Practitioner

In order to show you the origins of my image of myself as an imperfect therapist, I have to go back to the period in my twenties when

I was a professor at a small college in Alabama. When I moved on from there, it was with the hope that I would be joining a group of practitioners who were grounded in the realities of daily life. Enough of this ivory tower stuff about the way things are supposed to work; I wanted to find out how the world really is, and to do so in the company of other like-minded folks. Although initially I started out in solo practice, eventually I did find some companionship. When a friend and I created an outpatient clinic from scratch, we shared a vision that we could gather together a group of therapists who were not only expert clinicians but who were fun to be around. We carefully recruited those who we believed were the absolute best that our city had to offer—not only those who were well trained and successful but who brought in some playful energy and who had as their priority learning from one another.

The private practice of therapy is a lonely business, even more so than the work of other professionals. There is so much secrecy surrounding what we do. Between the scheduled hours and mandatory paperwork, there is actually little time for therapists to interact with others. The work environment is one of soundproofed walls, hushed tones in the office, and furtive glances in the waiting room. Unlike their colleagues who work in social service and community agencies, private practitioners are unrestrained by the bureaucracy of regular staff meetings. When those of us in our outpatient clinic did get together, it was often in a perfunctory way, more to discuss the pragmatics of collecting delinquent accounts than to help one another grow.

For a precious year or two, I did learn, and enjoy, what it is like to work with people you love to be around, folks you can go to for a hug when you need one. I was disheartened by the intellectual, spiritual, and professional limitations of private practice, where an emphasis is placed on getting clients to come back, to pay their bills on time, and to be grateful, rather than on actually helping them in the shortest feasible period of time, but at least I felt part of a caring group. However, there were other problems.

One of my major flaws is a tendency to see the best in people, to close my eyes to their faults and to contemplate only their most redeeming qualities. It is thus ironic that I am unwilling to do this with myself, setting personal standards that are so high I could never reach them with stilts much less my short legs, while I tend to give others the benefit of the doubt when I first meet them. Unfortunately, my partner was much like me, neither one of us being the hard-core business type. I suppose that is why we got along so well and wished to work together in the first place.

In spite of knowing that I was overly trusting, I never imagined just how much of my collegial support was an illusion. The dozen therapists who worked in our clinic were my friends. We went out for dinner together. We played with one another's children. We formed a united front, us against the slings and arrows hurled against us by the competition; Blue Cross, Blue Shield; and resistant clients.

Within a relatively short period of time, however, my partner and I were disturbed to discover that one of the therapists, one of our friends, was embezzling money from the clinic. She had been conspiring with her clients, having them pay her on the side so she would not have to report the income to us or the Internal Revenue Service. Considering that clients come to therapists in the first place because they often have problems with trust, roping such people into a conspiracy to defraud seemed unusually heinous.

If I had only known it, this was just the tip of the iceberg. We soon learned that another therapist was defrauding insurance companies by billing multiple sessions during the same hour. She would invite a family of four, say, to come in for an hour of treatment, then send out invoices as if she had seen each of the four separately. Insurance companies don't like this sort of thing, as you might imagine, so she was carted off to jail.

These therapists were dear friends of mine so it hurt all the more. It was not that I imagined these people were doing these strange things *to* me; rather what hurt was the feeling that I was such a bad judge of character that I had somehow missed their flaws. Considering that I earn my living making accurate assessments of character, this feeling of having misjudged was especially disorienting.

Then our first medical director was arrested for soliciting minors. He had been caught by an undercover policeman while hanging out in the restrooms of a local university. At least I had inherited him from others rather than hiring him myself, so I didn't blame myself too much for this imperfect judgment in hiring. Our second psychiatrist, however, fared no better: he had his license revoked for having sex with a patient.

Just when we were *really* questioning our judgment about people, we discovered another therapist was having sex with a client right in the office! He was actually charging money for these sessions. As I later learned when I testified against him, he forced her to keep a journal detailing their activities together over a period of years. I could not believe his immorality, and I was also stunned by his stupidity. This was a guy I had been working down the hall from for three years. I walked by his door each day and had no idea what was taking place on the other side.

Finally, the pièce de résistance, one of the best clinicians in the place, who had an impeccable reputation in the community, was discovered to have never finished graduate school and to have forged his license. For over ten years he had been operating as a therapist, and I might add, doing a pretty good job, without being licensed or qualified.

On My Own

By this time, I was feeling so discouraged and mistrustful, I left the clinic to go back into practice on my own. I had enough to worry about taking care of my clients and myself, much less monitoring the strange behavior of my colleagues. I figured I would find a nice, quiet spot where I could work without interruption or distraction. This was definitely the wrong move for someone who had already experienced a lifetime of professional isolation. During my doctoral years, the competition had been so fierce and the environment so poisonous I could not really trust anyone. During the five years I had spent in Alabama, I had nobody to talk to about my work, no colleagues to bounce ideas off, nobody to collaborate with. Then for the next several years, after our move back to Michigan, I had been so hungry for friendship that I hadn't been very discerning about whom I trusted.

Now here I was again, in a chamber of isolation. All day long, I did not see or talk to anyone other than my clients. I sat in my office and waited for representatives of the outside world to come to me, and troubled ones at that. Nevertheless, I endured it for a few more years, accumulating clinical experience that was to become the foundation for everything that I have written since then.

Burnout, or actually rustout, eventually set in, paralyzing me to the point where I felt utterly lost and hopeless. I became obsessed with failure. All my clients seemed resistant to me. I started making notes for what was to be a book on the subject of difficult cases. Its original working title was *Clients From Hell*, and it was about those people who drive therapists crazy. One of this book's prepublication reviewers got my attention by gently suggesting that I might have a problem with loss of compassion. The process of reconceptualizing the book (and renaming it *Compassionate Therapy*) helped me examine the state of my own dysfunction.

If I was a failure as a therapist, my clients didn't seem to know it. Most of them continued to improve, not so much in spite of me or because I was functioning on autopilot, but because I put so much of myself in my work. I may have been tired and discouraged, yet it was still crucially important for me to do good. Because I was overly concerned with my own imperfections, I drove myself even harder to make a difference in other people's lives. Then again, I saw a part of me in every client who walked through the door.

13

My Life in Every Session

I am fairly certain that most of us therapists choose a theoretical orientation and therapeutic style based primarily on our personal characteristics and unsatisfied needs. This is not to say that these reasons
are somehow undesirable or even illegitimate, just that it is difficult
to be honest about the true reasons why we operate the way we do.

In spite of their claims of intellectual integrity or the empirical
superiority of one approach over others, the therapists I know who
are overly concerned with establishing appropriate boundaries in
their work are often afraid of intimacy in their relationships. Further, those who are comfortable working exclusively on a cognitive
level, eschewing affective material as irrelevant, seem to be afraid
of their own feelings. Those clinicians who prefer to stay in the present or the past, who like confrontation or support, who adopt a
directive or a passive role, do so not only because it may be in the
best interests of their clients but also because it makes them feel
more comfortable.

I recognize that my desire for closeness with my clients and students is predicated on my firm belief that such a bond will help
facilitate trust and, therefore, encourage the risk taking that is so
necessary for change to take place. However, I also acknowledge
that my own personal needs for intimacy with a wide assortment of
people also motivate me to work in this way. I alternate between

periods of detachment and over-involvement, responding not only to a client's behavior but also to whisperings within me.

For many years, I put as much as I humanly could into my sessions. I vowed that I would not become the kind of therapist who is cut off from other people under the guise of objective detachment. But over a period of time, I began to violate this promise to myself. The stories that I heard were so wrenching and horrible that I shut myself down. I projected a shell of a person who pretended to listen. A young child would tell me about the emotional neglect she was suffering and the complete helplessness she felt about escaping her predicament. There was so little I could do for her, I stopped listening. An older woman with a faded numerical tatoo needed to tell the story of her youth in a concentration camp. I did all the appropriate things, but that wasn't really me in the room. Once this client started on the continuation of her narrative from the week before, I would lapse into my own fantasy, returning only when it was absolutely necessary.

Once a client was out of sight, he was out of mind. This, I was told, is the hallmark of the veteran. Like the surgeon who can make ghoulish jokes in between operations, or the lawyer who jests about the lives she holds in her hands, therapists too can listen to the most horrifying stories and then go about their business as if they just heard a weather report. I know this is the only way we could ever sleep at night. So many times I had told students that when you spend time thinking about your clients, it is not for them but for yourself. Your musing over their lives does not help them, so the question becomes what is it doing for you? What are you hiding from that you wish to distract yourself with the problems of others?

These are a few of the internal questions that have helped me to grow as a therapist, to confront my fears of intimacy and needs for closeness. Cutting myself off from my feelings toward and about my clients hasn't worked for me. The challenge has been for me to reach down deep to find love and compassion toward those people who go far out of their way to make themselves as unlovable as possible. It is not so much that I worry about my clients as that I am deeply

affected by them. I know how to separate myself from them, to distinguish between their issues and my own, it is just that I can find
some way to connect with almost everyone, and I don't always have
sufficient control over what comes through the line between us.

One of the reasons for this over-identification is that I see a part
of my life in every session. No matter how much I have worked on
myself, it seems as if I will always struggle with the same core issues
of self-acceptance, of feeling imperfect, and of the need for more
closeness in my life accompanied by the fear of rejection—although
I would like to think that I am making steady progress.

I start out with the best of intentions: *this* time I am going to
remain totally objective. A client begins speaking about his struggles in emancipating himself from his parents and I think to myself,
"Whew, at least I've got this one under control!" Then, somewhere
during the discussion, he mentions how much time he spends antic-
ipating how his parents will react to each of the decisions he makes.
I feel a familiar queasy sensation. I may not try to please my parents
any longer, but I sure spend a heck of a lot of time trying to win the
approval of their replacements in the form of mentors. Damn, I
think, there is nowhere to hide.

An adolescent girl speaks of her dream to be a professional
dancer. I breathe a sigh of relief, thinking that at least I have worked
through my own unrealistic fantasies. Then the doubts creep in.
Have I really given up my dreams? As this young woman continues
to speak about her frustration that nobody will take her seriously
(including me), I run through a collection of my own secret aspirations, some of which I have never even written in my journal much
less spoken aloud. At that exact moment, I have *become* this girl. I
am reliving all the times that I told somebody like me about what
I wanted to do with my life and received an indulgent chuckle in
return. I turn and face this young person fully. I now take her *very*
seriously.

A man talks about the emptiness of his life, the utter pre-
dictability of his existence. He knows just what he will be doing
tomorrow, the next day, next week, and so on throughout the rest

of the century. He challenges me to give him a date some time in the future. He will then tell me what he will be doing and where he will be doing it: "Let's see. 2004. You said a Tuesday morning in March? By then my oldest child will be in college. I probably got promoted by then to district manager. My wife and I will have sex about three times a month. No, by then it is probably down to twice a month. We still play bridge on Wednesday nights . . ."

I laugh out loud. What a life! I have a fleeting thought as his prediction continues to unfold, "Am I glad that my life is not so routine!" Or is it? I am only half-listening now as another part of me tries to predict where I will be and what I will be doing on a Tuesday morning in March of 2004. Certainly some of the projection is hazy, but I am alarmed by how much I can anticipate. So much for my illusions that I am in control of my destiny.

With each client and with every session I have ever been part of, there is so much time and room for me to personalize what is going on. I debate with myself as well as my students and colleagues whether this immersion of self in our work is altogether a good thing or too high a price to pay. I suppose some practitioners give themselves a choice in the matter when they *decide* to withhold themselves in their sessions. I only know that at the times when I have done that, I lose interest in the act of helping, which I am clearly not doing solely for the benefit of others but also to heal myself.

14

On Being a Hypocrite

I like to think that most of the time I am a pretty nice guy. I also perceive myself as a fairly effective therapist, having worked in this field for enough years to get a handle on my task. I mentally review some of the people I have helped over the years, to bolster my sense of competence. Surely I must know what I am doing if there is testimony from so many satisfied customers. I recall couples who walked in trying to throttle one another and left a few months later with a new sense of commitment to their relationship. I think of the hordes of adolescents, probably hundreds, who were on the verge of major self-destruction and now lead reasonably productive and satisfying lives, owing in no small part to my efforts. And then I envision all those depressed and anxious folks who made the pilgrimage to my office singly, in pairs, or with the whole clan and now feel much better about themselves and their lives.

So why do I feel like such a hypocrite?

Acting a Part

At least once a week somebody thanks me for something I have done for them. I take this as evidence that, at least occasionally, I am doing something right. This feedback feels great . . . for about fifteen minutes. I pat myself on the back and think to myself, "A job well done." Perhaps all the effort and aggravation are worth it if people are really affected by what I do. But then I start to feel a bit uneasy. Then downright sad. If only they knew what I was really like; what a hypocrite I am.

If the people I have helped only knew that while I may appear infinitely patient with them, I yell at my own son when he doesn't take out the trash; that even though I admonish families to spend quality time together, it is rare for my own family to eat dinner together; that I urge couples to make it a major priority in their lives to communicate their innermost thoughts, dreams, frustrations, and feelings to each other, yet my wife and I are so busy we barely catch up on what each of us did on any given day.

I feel like a hypocrite because I tell almost all of my clients to come to terms with their past, to put their families of origin in perspective, to loosen the bonds that strangle them every time they return home. I think of this in particular because I just returned from a trip to Michigan to visit my siblings, father, and grandmother (after two years between visits), and while I was back there I could not for a moment stop feeling like a martyr. I reverted back to the roles that made me nauseated as a child. Without losing so much as a beat, I rejoined the craziness that drove me away in the first place.

Perhaps you think it is unrealistic for me to expect otherwise. Maybe you believe that therapists are entitled to be a bit eccentric, even personally dysfunctional, as long as they do their jobs properly. But I seriously wonder if that is possible. Can I help people with aspects of life that I have not yet mastered? Can I help families resolve difficulties that I have not been able to take care of myself? Can I ask clients to do things that I cannot do?

I suppose one easy answer is that it depends on how accomplished an actor I am. Clients are, after all, so immersed in their own muck, so preoccupied with their pain and anguish, they often barely notice I am in the room. It would not take much for me to present the image of the omnipotent wizard, especially considering that this is exactly what many people wish me to be.

I appear to be someone completely in charge of his life. When onstage in my office, in the classroom, or before my colleagues, I am the embodiment of tranquility, confidence, and wisdom. I am all-knowing and all-loving. I am unflappable, charming, and compassionate. I am endlessly patient and never lose my temper. Yet inside, I often am filled with doubt. I second-guess myself, wondering if I know what I am doing or where I am headed. I barely know what to do with my own life, and yet here sits a person, or a whole roomful of folks, waiting for me to tell them what to do with their lives. Do these people realize how much I struggle simply trying to make a decision about what to order off a menu?

Every day, I preach the values of open communication, of taking risks, of breaking loose from the bonds of the past as if these are things that I am able to do and have regularly done. I talk about becoming independent of others' approval, of not needing to keep proving oneself, and yet here I am writing another book, this time peeling back every layer of my being to expose myself.

Do What I Say, Not What I Do

I hear a couple complain that they never seem to make enough effort to spend time with one another. I admonish them to reorient their priorities while I wonder to myself when my wife and I will do the same. A woman talks about her complex feelings regarding her relationship with her mother. When she does not see her mother for a while, she feels guilty; when she does go to visit, she feels abused by what she must put up with. Having just returned from my own trip to the past, still reeling from the stress of playing mediator, I tell her she is foolish for continuing to allow her mother to treat her as a child.

As if these examples from my caseload don't make me uneasy enough, I recall an instance in which I was lecturing to a group of graduate students on the importance of empathy in human relationships. This is a subject that I feel quite passionate about, so I put on quite a display of enthusiasm and excitement. I recited the literature and research supporting the value of compassion and car-ing in the effort to help someone. At the apex of my talk, I heard myself say, "How can you expect to help anyone if you cannot earn his or her trust and respect?"

The students nodded on cue. While so much of what they had learned in their training was often ambiguous, confusing, or abstract, this empathy stuff made a lot of sense. Everyone can recall how wonderful it feels to be totally accepted and understood by someone. The students even wrote this important message in their notes for later retrieval, in case it might be on their examination.

During the break, a student diffidently approached me, clutch-ing a sheaf of papers rolled up into a tight cylinder. "Dr. Kottler," she said, addressing me formally, "about this paper of mine you handed back. I really don't think this grade is fair." I could feel myself becoming defensive, all the while I was whispering to myself to stay calm, to not take this accusation personally, even though I felt that this person was questioning my judgment, my very com-petence as a professor. I quietly explained my rationale, pointed out the obvious deficiencies in her effort, and then dismissed her as if there was nothing left to discuss. Much to my surprise, the student continued to press her arguments, convinced that I had neither read her paper carefully nor understood what she was saying now. What I *did* hear was her challenging my judgment and integrity. As her voice became more shrill, mine took on an air of pompous indig-nation. By now, we had an audience of others who were nervously watching this exchange, averting their eyes in embarrassment.

Later, after I reflected on this encounter, what amazed me most was how blasé the other students appeared as they observed this heated conversation. Here was a professor who had just finished telling them how important empathy was in human relationships violating every one of the principles he had said were so crucial. It was as if they were used to seeing discrepancies between what their mentors said was important and what the mentors did in their lives. Whether they see the physician who is an overweight chain-smoker or the evangelist who seduces his congregants, people have become accustomed to so-called experts not following their own advice. Even though I may violate the principles that I consider most sacred, people are quite forgiving. This makes it so much easier to continue the hypocrisy.

Some Model I Am

As a therapist and teacher, I consider that one of the most important things I do, beyond any specific interventions or techniques, is to model those qualities and behaviors that I consider to be most desirable. If I wish family members to respond to one another more respectfully, I attempt to demonstrate respect in the ways that I interact with them. Likewise, I try very hard to show myself as someone who is willing to take risks, to reveal myself, to express myself clearly, to accept responsibility for my errors, to confront discrepancies, to respond with caring and directness. I like to think that the way I am with my clients is just as important as what I do with them.

Yet, in spite of the consistency with which I present myself in sessions as composed, serene, and confident, I recognize that I cannot practice in my life much of what I ask my clients to do. I do not mean to imply that I am not functioning at a fairly high level, or that my professional and family lives are not satisfactory, because they are, rather that I do not work on myself with the same dedication and zeal that I expect of my clients. There are, in fact, dozens of things that I hear myself say almost every week to families I see and therapists I supervise that I do not apply to my own life.

So what? you might ask. What unrealistic expectations I have for myself that I imagine I ought to be able to do what I ask of others! What difference does it make what I do in my personal life? What counts is what I do with the people I see in my office. Clients could not care less whether I have an unhappy marriage or a delinquent child or financial problems as long as these circumstances do not affect my work with them. Assuming that my private life does not affect my work (which I doubt very seriously), I nevertheless submit that being a hypocrite does compromise the effectiveness of my work, if not in the eyes of specific people I see, then in the image I present to the public.

There are few things that bother me more than hearing people complain about the marital therapist who can't seem to keep his own marriages together, the child therapist who can't control her own children, the family therapist who has failed to separate from his own dysfunctional family. It isn't that I disagree with the complainers, but that I know how accurate their complaints are. Sometimes, it seems almost every social gathering includes a few anecdotes about that crazy shrink who lives down the block. And all of us know a few experts in mental health who can barely function on a daily basis yet continue to see clients—and sometimes even appear to help them.

Reconciling the Real with the Ideal

"Michelle" and "Antonio" see me because they want to stop fighting so much. They appear to love one another, but they can't seem to get through a single day without one or the other fabricating some reason to begin a skirmish. As I talk with them, it occurs to me that whereas I spend an hour a week with this couple, engaged in the most intimate discussions of their innermost thoughts and feelings, I rarely do so with my own wife. Meanwhile, I'm lecturing Antonio about working too hard and not devoting enough time to his marriage, but by the way, it's 8:00 P.M., and I am still working myself. Michelle interrupts with a distracting comment. I become irritated, and feeling challenged, I tell her that she is upset with me (a projection if there ever was one). The session ends with me securing a commitment from both of them to spend at least thirty minutes a day talking about only things they appreciate about one another (the last time I did that with my wife was during our honeymoon).

Antonio and Michelle leave with a temporary truce that we all know will probably not last the drive home. I close up my office and put everything back in its place, like setting a stage for the next performance. I feel resolved to stop taking the people I love for granted.

Later that same night I am at home, writing these words. My son asks me to do something with him but I tell him, impatiently, to wait until later. I snap at my wife for not doing something the way I wanted. My son sits in his room behind a closed door, no longer interested in my company for now. I am exhausted and go to bed before I have a chance to have that heart-to-heart talk with my wife that I told Antonio and Michelle was so important.

When they come in for their next appointment, I want to confess that I didn't complete my homework either. But I don't. I act as if I am the embodiment of the fully functioning human being. A know-it-all. The perfect husband and father and friend. How can I go on with this sham, this hypocrisy? How can I continue to present this myth of being the consummate relationship specialist who knows exactly what is wrong with other people's lives?

I can't. Every time I hear from a client, a student, a supervisee, or a reader who expresses gratitude for my help, I not only feel elated, but sad and uncomfortable. I also feel motivated to reconcile the discrepancy between the image I project and the person I really am. I do not for a moment (well, maybe for a moment) actually believe that I can attain the level of personal functioning I aspire to. But what being in this field does most for me is push me to the limits of my capability as a human being as well as a professional. Every time I encounter a family who is struggling with an issue that is present in my own home, I feel an impetus to do something about that issue in my life to parallel the work the client and I are doing in our sessions. Every time a student or client asks for help in an area that I have not yet mastered, my feelings of hypocrisy strangle me until I at least try to reconcile the discrepancy.

Being a hypocrite is the part of me I despise the most. As long as I stay in this field, I have no choice except to continue to work on myself just as I continue to refine my clinical skills. I cannot any longer accept that it is all right for me to pretend to be compassionate, empathetic, logical, innovative, and direct with my clients if I am not willing to be this way with the people in my life whom I care about the most.

15

What Haunts Me

I love who I am when I am doing therapy. Who wouldn't? I am on my own turf, surrounded by books that remind me that I must know things. I am usually in a good mood; after all, I am being well paid for my time. This other person in the room with me usually shows proper deference. I love being called doctor, although I fiercely deny it and insist that I be addressed by my first name. I feel utterly in control. Although often I have no idea what a client is talking about or where things are going, I always appear to be in charge. When confused, I ask another question; the client assumes he or she has been unclear, apologizes, and tries again. When I have lost my place or have been daydreaming, I simply ask the client to summarize the essence of what has been expressed. Again, fault is somehow lodged once again in the client's domain: "Sorry for dragging on so long. What I mean to say is . . ."

I never get such breaks in my nonprofessional life. My son does not listen to me nearly as much as I would prefer. My wife listens to me, but I suspect that some of the time she is just pretending; she has heard it all before. Many of my colleagues don't pay much attention to me; they think me an eccentric but amusing crank; besides, they are planning their own rebuttals to whatever opinions I express. When I am with my brothers or other family members, they don't take me any more seriously than they did when I was twelve. Of course, I can *make* students listen to me but only with the threat that I will test them later on what I said. And then, as the converse of all this, there is what happens when I am being a therapist.

Clients appear to be spellbound by the least little statement that I offer; they feel so grateful and express their thanks enthusiastically. I don't wish to minimize the work that I do; I work very hard at being helpful to others. *That* is what I am saying. I try so hard to be a good therapist, to be influential and powerful, that I pretend to be someone that I am not. I am not nearly as patient or wise or caring as I appear to be in my office or classroom. I don't really know the answers to half the questions I attempt to address. Although I appear to be thoroughly unruffled by whatever transpires before me, inside I am actually quaking with apprehension and uncertainty. Of course, I can't tell anyone about these doubts because then *nobody* would ever listen to me again.

A client tells me that she hates me, that I am clearly the worst therapist who ever lived. She knows this for a fact, she quickly interjects before I have a chance to challenge the validity of her claim, because she has seen dozens of others before me. Further-more, she has a friend, well, more like an acquaintance, . . . ("Go on!" I am screaming inside my head. "Spit it out already!") who also knows me and thinks that I am a real loser. She looks at me smugly, as if to say, "Try to worm out of that one, you no good creep!"

I nod my head slowly. I wait several seconds, even a minute before I respond. I am perfectly still. I show absolutely nothing in my face or body. It is as if she just told me she likes my shoes. Finally, in measured tones and a silky voice that I am surprised betrays nothing of what I am feeling inside, I respond with the safest of ripostes, "You must be very angry to lash out like that."

While she is trying to wiggle away from that inviting morsel of bait, I consider the incongruence between what I am showing and what I am feeling. I am hurt. I am angry. Nibbling away at the edges of my performance, I can feel tremendous doubt, even despair. Whether she knows it or not, this client has nailed me in a major way: in my belief that no matter how much I learn and grow, I will always be mediocre in what I do. I thought graduating from college might change things. Ditto with getting a doctorate. Surely, writing a book would show I have *something* going for me. A dozen books later, I now know for certain (I am a slow learner) that this does not work either. No matter how much I accomplish, I can do nothing more than pretend to be self-accepting. After all, if I am trying to help others increase their self-worth, I had better at least *appear* reasonably satisfied with myself. If I am satisfied, however, why am I still such an easy mark for others who break right through my shell of security?

I have made tremendous progress in this area. As I have mentioned, one of the reasons I believe so strongly in the power of therapy is that I know how helpful a number of practitioners have been to me. They supported me when I did not feel capable of doing so by myself. They confronted the benefits I enjoy from staying the way that I am—imperfect and with good excuses for avoiding the hard work of changing. They helped me draw some connections between seemingly unrelated themes that had continued to haunt me. They encouraged me to venture out of my safe but self-defeating images of myself, to risk being more self-accepting. If you think that I have some work to do now, you should have known me earlier in my life when I was *really* insecure. At least now I know how to *pretend* to be confident. Most of the time, even *I* believe I know what I am doing, at least until somebody else finds a way to get through to that vulnerable core that I guard so well.

It is relatively rare for a client to get to me as thoroughly as the woman I just mentioned. With the help of a number of therapists, teachers, mentors, and family members, I am in reasonably good shape. I do know how to apply to myself those concepts that I teach others. As a result, I am almost always in a good mood and smiling. I rarely feel depressed or bored or empty. I absolutely love what I do for work, yet I find lots of time for adventure and play. During those infrequent intervals when I am dissatisfied with an aspect of my life, I am a fierce risk-taker, not at all afraid to make whatever changes are needed in order to revitalize myself.

Nevertheless, even with the internal stability and personal

control that I feel, I am tormented by a number of goblins that continue to haunt me: that one day I will go off the deep end and never return; that I will do something impulsive but spectacularly self-destructive; that I will have a stroke like my father and be trapped inside an immobile body; that all of sudden, one day I will wake up with nobody whom I love around; that I will work myself into such a financial and emotional debt that suicide will seem like a good idea; that I will realize I cannot escape death by creating works that I hope will make me immortal; that someone I love will betray me in such a way that I will never trust again. The list could go on and on, mostly variations of the same nightmare I have been living over and over again since graduate school.

My Familiar Companions

At the University of Virginia, there is an honor code similar to the one at West Point. We students were made to take an oath before every examination that we would neither give nor receive help, that as citizens of the university community we would not steal, lie, cheat, or otherwise act in a slovenly manner. If we were found guilty of any of these crimes, we had twenty-four hours to leave the university, with "Honor Code Violation" forever branded on our transcripts. The joke was that we should always keep a bag packed underneath our beds, just in case.

I never found this very funny. Even years after I left the university, I had a reoccurring nightmare in which I was awakened in the middle of the night by an urgent banging on the door. There, standing before me, were the members of the Honor Committee, dressed in somber academic robes, come to ask me to return my diploma. Retroactively, they have discovered that I have lied, that my supposed expertise is fraudulent. This is the core issue that haunts me the most of all.

Considering that most of my goblins dwell within the territory of teaching, counseling, writing, it is a wonder that I have not

retired from these endeavors that force me to confront over and
over again that which I fear the most. But then again, I said I liked
taking risks. I like it when my heart beats fast. I like jumping off
bridges, out of airplanes, into caves, along reefs, down glaciers, as
long as I can be reasonably certain the safety device (bungee cord,
parachute, rope, scuba gear, skis) is easily within my control. When
I am facing a new adventure or an old nemesis, I feel completely
alive, as if each of my heartbeats doubles the length and intensity
of my existence.

That is why I continue to teach, write, and do therapy even
though I am occasionally and unpredictably terrified by the doors
that they open. Just when I arrogantly believe that I have everything under control, that I know exactly what is at stake and what
recurrent issues might be triggered, *wham*, I am broadsided from a
direction I could never have anticipated.

My core issues, at least the ones I am aware of, are as familiar to
me as the geography of my own face. I recall leading a group in
which the theme of gender issues emerges. One of the women con-
fesses that she has never really trusted men; that is why she keeps
siding with a few of the other female group members even when
they are engaging in self-destructive behavior, "We have to stick
together." I very carefully bring the dysfunctional aspects of this
interactional style to her attention and, perhaps not surprisingly,
she becomes defensive. And then angry.

"Oops," I think. "What did I do wrong?" I have problems with
anger. Big time. I hate it when people are angry at me. I hate it even
when I know that a client is not really angry at me but at the person I remind her of. I tell myself that the woman is now acting out
exactly what she said was her problem—resentment towards men.
"Nah," I think. "I am letting myself off the hook too easily. Yes, I
am a man, but I also have some responsibility for this conflict
between us." Don't I? I don't know. As I mentioned, I have a hard
time functioning very well when anger comes up. I usually don't
even let clients get to the point where they become angry. I tell

them that anger is a useless emotion (to me, anyway) and why not look at what they are doing inside themselves to make themselves so upset? This usually works quite well.

In addition to my unfailing recognition of an "anger alert," I also recognize other issues as soon as they rear their heads; they are related to my needs to be perfect and to escape from mediocrity and to my restless adventurousness, my search for intimacy, and my essential aloneness. I not only know what these core issues are but I know how to hide from them. One of the side effects of being therapists is that we become skilled at playing games with ourselves, and others, if that is our intention.

I notice, for example, that at this very moment there is a raging debate inside my head whether I should trek across old ground once again or draw a new map and redefine it or venture forward into unknown territory. With great reluctance, I move forward, ducking along the way. I face a similar struggle every time I do anything more than once. After teaching the same course or workshop two dozen times, I know what will generate the most interest, the greatest laughter, the most provocative responses. If I deviate from The Plan, I do so at the risk of unknown and unpredictable results.

When I do therapy as well, I have the choice of sticking with a time-tested, structured, and reliable method that has worked before, or I can operate more intuitively and spontaneously and be more process oriented. When I rely on the former method, I feel more control (and impose more limits on what can happen); when I try the latter, I can not only facilitate moderate progress but sometimes also something quite spectacular. I do so, however, not only at the client's risk but at my own.

A client and I were humming along, for example, following our usual routines. Each week, he presented another in a series of dilemmas he faced at work, with his parents, and in his never-ending search for a lover. I had discovered what worked fairly well for him. I would let him talk himself out, interrupting to clarify or draw connections to previous themes as needed. I would then ask him what he needed to do differently. He would tell me, then give excuses why he couldn't do these things just yet. I would agree with him, having found that more direct confrontation elicited only more entrenched resistance from him. He then would make a commitment to take one step in the direction he desired; after which I would support him enthusiastically. This process was relatively easy for both of us; we both knew what to expect, and we both got something out of the exchange. The client observed steady and modest progress, while I felt reassured that I was doing something useful.

Perhaps out of boredom with the routine, or (I would like to think) because I sensed there was a better way, I decided one day to risk our usual course for another tack that might gather more momentum. I shared more of myself with him that day, revealing my hunch that we were both taking the path of least resistance. I told him I suspected that we might continue on this journey indefinitely, making steady and unremarkable progress even if we covered essentially the same territory over and over again. It was at this point that I realized I was speaking to myself as much to him.

This client, who so desperately wanted my support, readily agreed to try some variations on our usual plan, although I sensed that he was doing so more for my approval than for any passionate interest in accelerating our work. I wanted his cooperation on any terms, although at the time I had no idea why this change in our relationship was so important. In any case, he proved to be an able student of change, intensifying his commitment to the process. After taking more risks with one another, disclosing things that we had each held in abeyance, not wanting to hurt the other's feelings, remarkable changes began to take place within a short period of time. He quit his job and started his own company. He ceased all contact with his parents until he could see them on his own terms. Best of all, he stayed in a difficult relationship with a woman rather than fleeing as he was prone to do previously.

As all of this action took place, I began to feel more and more envious of him, if not downright resentful. With our newfound

openness, I snapped at him one time, accusing him a little too zealously of being irresponsible and impulsive. He wondered aloud if I
was not overreacting a bit. Teasingly, he suggested I was jealous. He
was right.

Change Junkie

As I described earlier, after ten years of practicing therapy full-time,
the last several years on my own, I felt stuck. I experimented with
different methods, various office arrangements and specialties, each
alteration buying me a little time before I hit bottom again. It might
take a few years or only a few months, but eventually all my clients'
stories began to sound the same. My areas of research focused on
failure and negative outcomes. After a brief respite of delving into
how and why so many divergent helping methods are equally effective, I once again became obsessed with difficult clients. At one
point, it seemed that all the people I saw were difficult. They were
belligerent, resistant, overly compliant, boring, empty, dependent,
or depressingly hopeless.

I dreamed of a different life, one in which I moved back into the
domain of academia. I felt myself moving full circle. Years before, I
had left my teaching position in Alabama to challenge myself on
another level. Now I felt that I could keep living the same comfortable but empty life until I died. Would that really be so bad, I
wondered? Don't most people settle into a rhythm in their lives,
essentially repeating the same routines each day? Was I running
away from being a responsible adult every time I moved on to something else?

Yet I also wondered if my wanderlust was not a gift. It does take
a certain amount of courage as well as discomfort with the status
quo to give up the good life and start over. I might or might not
have had the courage, but the dissatisfaction was awfully present for
me. Yet I could feel my reluctance to act, too. I had even more
excuses than my client as to why a move was not possible. I couldn't

afford it. Nobody would want me. I could not uproot my family. I was too old to make such a change, too comfortable in my life-style. Haunting me most of all were the voices of my father and a therapist I consulted who accused me of being irresponsible and fleeing when things become difficult: "That is your trademark, Jeffrey. You jump into something with both feet, root around a little, and just when things get a little tough, you run away. When are you going to grow up?"

I *am* a change junkie. Since I was seventeen, I have never lived in the same house for more than a few years. I change cars as often as most people have them waxed. I constantly fantasize about travel and am always just coming back from somewhere exotic or on my way there. Furthermore, in everything except my marriage and friendships, I have lived by the credo that no matter how good life is, it's probably better somewhere else. I have tested this hypothesis every chance I get.

I became a therapist, in part, so I could enjoy other people's changes vicariously. Every week, I help launch into the world dozens of people who go out and do wonderful and exciting things they have always wanted to do, then they come back and report to me how things went. I even get to ask questions.

If I were my own client, I would ask myself what I am afraid of. I would wonder not only what I am searching for, but what I am avoiding. If I refused to use my therapeutic ploys to hide, if I tried to be as honest as I am able, I would plead guilty to a need to stay in motion. At first, I believed that I was afraid of myself, and as I do with so many subjects I am interested in, I decided to write a book, this time on the subject of private moments and secret selves. From the thousands of interviews I conducted with others about how they deal with their solitude, I learned that in comparison I am a virtual hermit. I *like* being alone. I enjoy my own company and cherish such time whenever I can steal it.

If I am not afraid of myself, then what am I searching for so obsessively that I feel the need to turn my life upside-down every few years? When things become comfortable and secure, why do I venture off into the wilderness, subjecting my family and myself to hardships and the trauma of readjustment? What haunts me so persistently that I move onward, hoping "it" never discovers my forwarding address?

At about this time in my decision-making struggle (about seven years ago), I accepted another new client. Like most of the people I work with these days, she is also a therapist. I like seeing therapists as clients because that way I can get even closer to the flame. They are notoriously impatient and demanding. Yet things also move along more quickly because the client and I can speak in code. Since we both know the same rules and language, we can skip the foreplay and get right down to the heart of the matter.

This particular therapist was suffering from the aftereffects of getting too close to some of her clients; she had been burned badly, so much so that she decided not to do this kind of work any longer. During the process of putting her pieces back together, I hear her ask the same question that has haunted me throughout the years: "What the heck do I want to do before I die?" This triggers for me a core issue that grabs me in the groin and won't ever let go. If the fear that I will turn out not to know what I am doing is the core issue that haunts me the most, this is the core issue that frightens me the most. It is the theme that I most dread in my conversations with clients, and unfortunately, it comes up quite a lot. I am speaking, of course, about the existential theme of the fear of death. This is my favorite teaching metaphor, the one where I instruct the members of the audience to put their hands on their hearts, to feel this fragile muscle beating away, second after second, their lives literally hanging on the whims of this organ that is slowly, irrevocably wearing out.

My own impending death is terrifying for me. Whereas others may find solace in believing in an afterlife or in spiritual transcendence or in hiding from the subject altogether, pretending that the time of death is far away, none of these strategies have worked for me. I am convinced that I will not live to a ripe old age.

Most certainly, my life is more than half over. When my parents were about my age my mother was dying of cancer and my father's arteries were closed so tight that even coronary bypass surgery could not prevent a stroke. Surely, no matter how careful I am about what I eat and how zealously I exercise every day, I cannot undo my genetic inheritance. Every day I take a shower and watch my hair going down the drain, I am reminded that I am slowly dying. Every time I read a menu, I remember that this is as healthy as I will ever be; it's all downhill from here on out. Since my bladder now wakes me up a few times each night, I have a lot more time to think. It was hard enough to fall asleep once each night; now I often tackle that challenge several times a night, each effort presenting a different set of disturbing images.

I treat each day as if it were my last. Although I make plans constantly about what I hope to do tomorrow, next week, or next month, I rarely forget that this is wishful thinking. I certainly expect to live several more years, and I hope, a few more decades, but I will not be surprised if my number is called early. In any case, I prefer to assume that I don't have much time left. I would feel really terrible if I died with regrets about things I wish I had done. I can honestly say that there are few such things, and if I could think of one right now, I would make plans to do it quite soon.

I feel bad for my therapist client. She has no passion in her life. She is playing out her cards as if she can't reshuffle and draw another hand. She acts as if what she has and does is all that she will ever know. I shake my head in wonderment. What is it that she really wants, I ask her, "Love? . . . Excitement? . . . A different job or career? . . . More education? . . . A change in locale? . . . So, what stops you from having any of the things you want?"

She doesn't know what she wants. We sit silently, ignoring one another for the moment as we each consider our own thoughts. I suspect she is feeling sorry for herself, because I am feeling a little that way myself. It occurs to me that I am not sure what I want either.

This image of not living up to the same standards I set for my clients really gets underneath my skin. I begin to itch so badly I can no longer ignore the discomfort. I am no longer willing to be an imperfect therapist. If nothing else, I will launch myself into a new arena, one that affords me the opportunity to heal myself even more powerfully. I realize I cannot do this alone, nor are my loving family and a skilled therapist at my side enough support for me to venture forward. Like an alcoholic who must change his whole environment in order to make major life-style changes, I realize I must get away from the place where I was born and all the ghosts that reside there. I must find a place with the kinds of opportunities that will allow me to continue to grow, not only as a therapist but as a human being.

I take a deep breath, and I jump. I call a family meeting and explain to my wife and son that I want to look for an academic position once again. I am tired of being a therapist in the way I have been living and functioning. I want to try teaching again, a decision that means we must move away from our extended family in Michigan. To my surprise, my wife is supportive even though it means she will leave behind her friends and family and that she will have to help me soften the blow to our son, who is devastated. Little did we realize that his grief and tears would last a full two years.

In retrospect, I didn't feel that I had much of a choice. It was move on and continue growing as a professional and human being or die slowly. Within a period of six months, I was involved in three serious car accidents, the last of which I barely escaped alive. I began to wonder if this was because I was distracted, perhaps even severely depressed or acting out a death wish. In any of these cases, I had to do something. I had to get away again from the place where I was born if I was ever going to find my way. I had to restructure my life in such a way that I could move forward, even if it meant living with my son's tears.

Part VI

Perfectionistic Teacher

16

Between Legends and Lies

A significant part of my growth as a therapist and a trainer of therapists has resulted from the sheer diversity of places that I have worked. I have always searched for an environment that would supply the kind of support and stimulation that I have been hungering for my whole life. Unfortunately, either my standards have been unrealistic or I have made some poor decisions about where to go. As I mentioned earlier, one other piece of this puzzle I don't like to acknowledge is that I become bored easily, and rather than investing the hard work involved in confronting the source of my inertia, I prefer to move somewhere else to start over again.

There are a few other reasons why I made the transition from practitioner back to academician, or at least reasons that I told myself and that are an approximation of truth. Probably the most obvious of these was simply that I believed that, with sufficient persistence, I now might find a teaching position somewhere. One of the strongest driving forces for me is the need to make a difference with the greatest number of people. If I get a rush from reaching a single client during a moment of insight, it is infinitely more satisfying to reach a dozen, a hundred, or even a thousand people.

More than once the thought has occurred to me that if I mentor a single faculty member who in turn influences hundreds of future therapists who themselves will each influence hundreds of other clients, I have the opportunity to make a notable mark on my small part of the world. The life of a teacher, therefore, seemed like a logical objective for me to move toward after I grew disenchanted with full-time practice.

Student to Teacher

I have never forgotten what it was like to be a student; in many ways, this has been my greatest strength as a teacher. I remember sitting in my elementary school classes, staring at the clock that never seemed to move, counting the minutes until I was free. I recall enduring the days of high school, wondering what algebra was for, much less what the sense was of those strange symbols. How would this help me get a girlfriend? How would it make my parents stop fighting? How would it stop me feeling so bad about myself and my life?

Elementary and secondary teachers are usually trained rather than grown.. They take a series of courses in how to write lesson plans, use technological aids, operate audiovisual equipment, design bulletin boards, and construct tests. They learn how to manage classrooms, institute discipline procedures, and initiate cooperative learning groups. Yet even with all this education, children often wonder why it is that teachers understand so little about how real learning takes place.

But college and university professors are another breed altogether! We have received virtually no preparation in how to teach others about our areas of expertise. It is assumed that because we are specialists in our fields we can explain what we know to others so that they can apply this knowledge. If this is really the case, why do the best teachers seem to be the ones who make complex ideas accessible by going beyond their specialties and drawing together ideas and metaphors from many sources? Earlier, I talked of how dissatisfied I was in graduate school. I found most of my professors to be dull and out of step with what was going on in the real world. Many of the classes I was required to take had absolutely nothing to do with helping people; they were designed more as hoops for us students to jump through to prove we were worthy of joining the ranks of an exclusive club. In one of my most crucial courses on helping skills, the instructor carried a little notebook in which he rated the depth of our questions and the profundity of our comments, even when we were just chatting about ideas we were confused about. Rather than learning how to relate to others in an authentic manner, we were taught to memorize a list of appropriate responses to most any utterance of distress. The little marks in the instructor's notebook somehow figured into our final grade and took on a significance to us far greater than any course content.

Running to the Battle or Away from It?

When I first worked with little kids, I learned how critical it was to have their attention if I expected to teach them anything. The first and most important thing any teacher can do is present himself or herself in such a way that other people want to hear what he or she has to say. This was certainly not the case with the instructor just described—we were all so concerned with earning the right little marks in his notebook that we rarely considered we were actually there to learn some important skills.

I have never forgotten this lesson from my years as a student and as a nursery school teacher: unless I can keep students' interest, unless they believe that I offer them something they really need, they may humor me, but they will never really learn what I have to offer. That is why my drive to be a perfect teacher always falls short. That is why I have kept moving onward, trying to find a better place that might inspire me to reach my true potential.

This last part sounds so noble, as if I am sacrificing myself, my comfort, the very stability of my family life, all in the service of others. I don't buy this any more than you do—but you have to admit it sounds good. The painful fact of the matter is that I run from conflict just as those little nursery school kids ran themselves in circles until they were too dizzy and tired to continue.

I pout when I don't feel appreciated. In the various teaching jobs I have had, there has been a recurrent theme; it is like a chorus in my life. I try to work harder than anyone else, put more of myself into what I do, in order to prove (more to myself than to others) that I am worthy. I am usually successful in my efforts.

When someone works as hard as I do to be good at something, there is an inevitable result—many consumers and colleagues will greatly appreciate his or her efforts. And some won't. You would think that I might be realistic enough to settle for this reasonable and predictable state of affairs. However, being perceived to be or actually functioning at a less than perfect level gnaws at me. I start to blame others for not appreciating me to the extent that I deserve. I seem to draw the wrath of the traditional constituency, who find me in some ways unpleasant (I prefer the term "threatening," but I may be dreaming).

The way this scenario has unfolded time and time again is that some older member of the staff, usually someone in a position of power and authority, does not like the way I operate. Perhaps not coincidentally, I tend to get a lot of attention as a result of being reasonably successful at my teaching and writing. This reputation does not seem to enhance my esteem in this person's eyes. I can feel his or her scorn. Being as oversensitive to conflict as I learned to be growing up on an emotional battlefield, I don't seem to be able to tune out what is often more an annoying distraction than a serious impediment to my doing my job. Instead, my pattern has been to become indignant. I wait until some major injustice has occurred, usually one in which I have been slighted or undermined. Then I say to myself, "Screw it! Who needs this aggravation. I am going somewhere I can be appreciated." Then my family and I pack our bags and move on.

To be fair, truth is somewhere between my legends and my lies. I *have* seemed to invite a lot of petty jealousy from some who find me threatening. I *do* seem to draw more than my share of attention, a circumstance that provokes resentment. Yet I also orchestrate

things in such a way that, inevitably, I will feel let down. My expectations for feeling appreciated have been so out of line with what is
reasonable that disappointment is almost always likely. The truth is
that I *like* to move a lot and start over. When I am looking for an
excuse to do so, there is a familiar one available that I have learned
to recognize.

Back to the Story

In moving from practitioner back to academician, I wished to recap-
ture the joy I had once felt as a full-time teacher. I kept remember-
ing how exhilarated I felt the very first time I was given my own
class to do with whatever I wanted.

My first teaching assignment was as a doctoral student at the
University of Virginia. As part of my assistantship, I was sent to
Quantico Marine Base to teach an introductory counseling class to
a bunch of marine colonels who, on the verge of retirement, were
looking for a new career (as counselors yet!). I walked in that first
day, a twenty-four-year-old novice with long curls hanging over my
collar, only to face this room full of marine colonels sitting at attention. They called me sir, but they looked at me with confusion and
uncertainty. Theoretically, I was a kind of superior officer, someone
who held the power to evaluate their performance, but I sure didn't
look like anything they had ever saluted.

I reveled in the control I wielded. These guys, twice my age with
triple the life experience, deferred to me. They did so not only
because of my position but also because I knew things that they
didn't know. I would casually mention that they might read something of interest, and the next week they had practically memorized
the material. I would tell them about the simplest of concepts (to
me), that their relationships with family members and friends would
improve dramatically if they would only concentrate on listening
more and talking less. And that if they did talk, expressing what was
in their hearts was just as important as saying what was in their

heads, especially if they could do so without appearing like marine colonels. As they practiced these skills and noted their effects, my esteem in their eyes rose almost to the level of my invisible rank. It was the very beginning of sensing my own power to influence others. This was also the best part of my graduate program.

However, in keeping with the theme I described earlier, I had a hard time with a few members of the faculty. Most of these conflicts were my own doing. I was in a hurry. I had decided that I wasn't learning very much anyway, so I might as well get the hell out of there as soon as I could. I plotted and planned a way to get my doctorate in record time. I had finished my dissertation before my first semester, loaded myself up with courses, and figured out how to breeze through the system. Clearly, this impatience and drive did not endear me to some of my professors, who had the audacity to believe that I was there to learn something, that I should take my time and savor the experience. Frankly, I couldn't figure out what was there that I was supposed to learn.

This was a time before sexual harassment was clearly identified and labeled, before it was considered out of line for professors and students to have multiple relationships—as protégés, friends, and even lovers. While initially I was jealous of the intimate relationships that developed between some female students and their male advisors, giving these students access to opportunities that I envied (going to conventions with advisors, whispering words with them in the hallway, meeting clandestinely, and so forth), eventually my turn came. A gay faculty member "hit" on me. I politely declined the invitation, and he did what he could to get me booted out of the program. If my own advisor had not been powerful enough to neutralize this effort, I would never have been permitted to graduate.

As I relive this episode, I hardly feel embittered. On some level, I believe I was asking for trouble. I make a good target. If only I could learn to fit into the mold that has been set for me by others, I wouldn't invite this kind of retribution. As hard as I have tried to be modest, self-deprecating, quiet, and unassuming, I come across as a smartass know-it-all. Naturally, that is going to anger some people, especially those in positions of power. There is some hindsight here on my part; some events and results that may seem obvious to you I have not understood until fairly recently. It has taken me about five re-enactments of this scenario (and writing a book on the subject of blaming others during interpersonal conflict) to become willing to assume responsibility for my role in these struggles.

Exiled in Alabama

I received my Ph.D. at a time when jobs in academia were especially tight. I was delighted, therefore, that anyone called me for an interview, although I was a little leery that the people on the other end of the line were in Alabama. Didn't they lynch Jews in Alabama? I seemed to recall that the world headquarters for the Ku Klux Klan was about ten miles from the town where I would live.

My wife and I located Alabama on the map between Mississippi and Georgia, a vast region of the country in which nobody I knew had ever set foot. They had mosquitoes down there, I had heard, lots of them, as well as the people running around in white sheets, talking funny. When I arrived in Florence, Alabama, a newly minted Ph.D. looking five years younger than my twenty-five years, I was impressed that they treated me like a grown-up. They seemed to want me, for some reason I couldn't fathom, so my wife and I decided to give it a chance.

I could not have chosen a more ideal setting in which to learn to be a teacher. Whereas in major institutions the job of a faculty member is more to conduct research than to help students, at this small college they were suspicious of anyone who might wish to write—it just took time away from the classroom. Also, there is not much to do in that "dry" county located an hour's drive from even the small city of Huntsville, so there was plenty of time to read books, talk to colleagues, and concentrate on being the best teacher I possibly could. I decided humor was a critical part of teaching. So was being kind and sensitive toward students, treating them as if they were the most important people in the world to me, which I felt they were.

Since there was so little urging by the administration for teachers to do or be anything in particular, I generated a lot of internal pressure to excel. It wasn't enough for me to be a good teacher; I needed to be the absolute best. Part of this pressure came from my now familiar neurotic strivings to prove I was worthy of being in my position; the other part, just as important, was my desire to be what teachers had never been for me. I wanted to make school fun, and I couldn't imagine anything more thrilling than learning to be a therapist. There is no other field I can think of in which every class can spark personal growth as well as professional development. Students should leave each day armed not only with some understanding about what people are like, why they defeat themselves, and how to be most helpful to them but also with the potential to apply this awareness to themselves. I not only permitted such opportunities but encouraged them.

As much as I enjoyed my time in north Alabama, I also felt in exile. I was out of the mainstream, far away from a decent library, much less any professional support. There were only two of us in the department, and since my colleague defined therapy basically as praying with her clients, we didn't have a lot in common. I learned lots from my friends in geography, political science, nursing, and English, but I had nobody to talk to in my own field.

These were my formative years as a teacher, and I lived them alone. I felt darn lucky to be working at all, so I stayed as long as I could, trying to stay current in my field even though most of the time I ended up talking to myself. With so few opportunities to interact with other professionals, I had a lot of time to figure out what I believed about helping people.

Perhaps my capacity for creativity was even ideally suited to this isolated environment. Since I was definitely not in the mainstream, I felt free to explore alternative ways to think about therapy and education. I felt uninhibited and unrestrained about asking what seemed to me at the time to be rather obvious questions: How does the therapist change as a result of being a change agent for others? How do members of this profession deal with their doubts, imperfections, and inadequacies? How is it possible that practitioners can operate in such different ways and yet produce similar results? What are the things we know for sure about the ways people change? What are the human dimensions of helping others?

With few colleagues to bounce ideas off, I began a mostly solitary quest in search of answers to the questions that plagued me. My dialogues were silent ones as I mentally debated with the authors I read, struggling to make sense of the paradoxes involved in helping others: how the therapeutic relationship is intimate and authentic yet also contrived; how it attempts to foster independence by temporarily perpetuating dependence; how it is supposed to be a safe and secure setting but can also be quite dangerous. These paradoxes and polarities made me dizzy with confusion, and yet I had few people to help me make sense of them.

I was restless and antsy but didn't quite have the courage to make a change. My wife and I had just created a son who was only a few weeks old when we decided to move on. Like so many of the decisions I have initiated in my life, this one was impulsive as well.

Learning to Speak from My Heart

In a single afternoon one year before our departure, when I had been feeling especially restless, I had scribbled off a grant application to the International Communication Agency, an organization that sponsors Fulbright Scholars on trips abroad—structured adventures to educate underdeveloped nations.

When the letter announcing my award unexpectedly arrived, I was dumbfounded. Here I was, a tenured professor with a mortgage, a family to support, and an idyllic life on the banks of the Tennessee River. I decided to accept the award anyway. Then my application for a sabbatical was denied as was my subsequent request for an unpaid leave. It seems I was so indispensable they were unwilling to part with me for a year. So I quit.

The situation was further compounded by the reality that when I had submitted my application, I had checked Peru as my first choice. Since Peruvians speak Spanish and the job involved teaching and consulting, I was required to have my fluency in Spanish certified by a qualified person. That seemed reasonable. I visited my friend who was chair of the Language Department and asked if he would fill out my form. He asked me if I spoke Spanish. "*Sí*," I replied with a shrug of my shoulders. *No problema.* He was delighted to help. The problem now was that *sí* was about all I could remember from my high school Spanish. If I chose to accept this invitation, I had five months to become fluent enough in Spanish to teach in it. No problem. I can do this. The only reason I didn't do well in Spanish before was that I had no motivation. Now I had a reason to study.

We did go to Peru for six months, and I did learn Spanish well enough to get along and do my job. As I look back on this adventure, I am reminded that what made it happen was my willingness to take a leap of faith. I had never been a good student of language, but I figured that if it was important enough to me I could do most anything. This is neither arrogance nor delusion. It is simply the claim of an ordinary person who badly wants to escape his own mediocrity.

While in Peru, I was assigned to teach in several institutions in Lima, one of which was known as "the Communist university," the place where the terrorist organization Shining Path was born. It took several months before I could meet my first class, since the university was almost always on strike. Meanwhile, I occupied myself doing research with witch doctors in the jungle. One of the psychiatrists attending my seminar for professionals in the community invited me to join him on a trek to one of the most remote villages in this part of the world, a place that was considered to be the capital of sorcery in that region. We took a plane, then a bus, finally hopping onto the back of an old truck that was dropping off supplies for the week.

I stayed in the home of a young, up-and-coming witch doctor, who introduced me to the eldest practitioner in the village. Although this practitioner had never met anyone with my skin and eye color, he was impressed that I was a healer from across the water. When I used some of my magic to cure his headaches, which were probably the result of ingesting too many hallucinogenic drugs during his healing rituals, he invited me to study with him. (I simply taught him some basic meditation breathing techniques, complete with his own mantra.)

I joined Don José on his very next healing processional. A dozen of us hiked to the top of a mountain where we spent the long night chanting, dancing, telling our stories, and letting him work us over with his spells. He also blew a mescaline-like substance up our nostrils, a singularly unpleasant experience that produced a vomiting reflex. The object was to purge our bodies of the evil spirits that had invaded our souls. When, as a parting gift, Don José gave me a magic potion designed to protect me from further spiritual infections from my clients, I had the barest glimmerings of an idea that I was later to develop into a series of four books about how therapists are affected and influenced by their clients, invaded as it were, by clients' pain and anguish.

Some time after this, I finally began my first class at the university. We met in a building that resembled something one might see in Beirut. The windows were all smashed in, and angry graffiti scrawled on the walls. There were posters of Lenin and Marx plastered on the buildings, a statue of Che Guevara out front. Here I was to talk to them about U.S. therapeutic methods, yet America was a dirty word.

I have never had more fulfilling experiences as a teacher than those I encountered in this hotbed of dissent and at the dozen other places I worked in Peru—a women's college, a university for the country's elite, a medical school, and various community groups and professional organizations. I also discovered, to my amazement, that while conversing in the Spanish language I had another personality, one that was more flamboyant and emotional. Since I had fewer words as my disposal to describe the complex process of therapy, I learned to be more expressive with my face and body. Even after I returned home, I retained this penchant for "body English," using as much of myself as I can when I speak, to communicate what is inside me. I learned to speak not only from my head but from my heart.

Juggling Lives

Teaching in Peru sparked in me a greater commitment to work with people who needed help the most rather than just those who found my services most accessible. But since at this time I was returning to the life-style of private practice in an affluent suburb of Detroit, the gnawing feeling that I was hiding from my responsibility to help the more needy people never left me, and it did eventually urge me back into public service.

While working as a psychologist in the settings I described earlier, seeing fifteen to twenty people per week, I had tried to juggle that career with another career in the classroom. Since academic positions had all but dried up for white males during these important years of affirmative action, I had satisfied myself with teaching part-time at two quite different institutions. By far the more interesting of the two was a free-standing institute dedicated to "growing" humanistic therapists rather than "training" them, as traditional universities do.

At this center, the emphasis was on the personal dimensions of being a therapist rather than on intellectual content or clinical skills. I found this refreshing, even if it made me a little uneasy that my students had some distinct problems adapting their style to situations and settings where this approach was hardly appropriate. In one of the courses I taught, Intuition, Power, and Enchantment, we explored the more subtle aspects of change processes. We visited museums to study symbols in works of art. We spent a day on cross-country skis in the woods, accessing our powers of intuiting and enchanting as a group. We worked together to develop each person's capacities as a healer of self and others.

As intriguing as this method of growing therapists sounds, I also felt uneasy with its lack of structure and overly flexible boundaries. Eliminating grades and fostering an atmosphere of trust and openness were indeed wonderful as concepts, but their execution turned out to be a problem for me. Some of the students attracted to an alternative program such as this operated on the fringe of respectability; the same could be said for a few of the faculty as well. Also, as much as I enjoyed the freedom that pervaded the old mansion where classes were held, some of the expressed warmth felt contrived and artificial. I enjoy a hug as much as the next person, but hugs lose their feeling of specialness when they become as casual as handshakes. The usual form of greeting one another and of beginning and ending a meeting or class at this institute was a round of hugs. I don't like to hug anyone and everyone just because it is expected.

In marked contrast to this strange but lovely setting for growing therapists, I was also teaching conventional counseling courses at a local university, using lectures, examinations, discussions, and such, as was consistent with the atmosphere of this program. My students were quite bright and did very well in their academic tasks, also showing a high degree of competence in their clinical skills. What worried me the most, however, was a theme I was to continue to ponder: some of these folks may have known their stuff but they sure couldn't apply it to themselves. I wondered if there might not be some way to bring about a compromise between these two extreme positions, but there was no chance of doing so as long as I remained a part-time participant. It became to clear to me that if ever I was going to have any real influence in shaping an academic program, I would have to reenter academia on a full time basis. I wanted, no I *needed*, to be a teacher full-time.

Atten-hut!

Among the academic job offers I had once I decided to leave private practice was an intriguing opportunity to be a program coordinator. Finally, I would have the position and the clout to create the kind of atmosphere I had always searched for. I could hire faculty who had similar goals. I could shape the department to be the prototype of perfection I had always wanted. The situation seemed perfect. A small college in a gorgeous part of the country. Antebellum homes. Tropical weather. Oh, yes. Did I mention that the job was at The Citadel? Did I say that I would have to wear a uniform (I would have the rank of major), that my program would be ensconced in a military institution that denied entrance to women except during the dead of night?

I must have been hypnotized by visions of life in Charleston, clearly one of the most picturesque spots on Earth. I must have been seduced by promises of autonomy. I must have been demented. This experiment lasted but a few months before I realized the magnitude of my mistake. The students were wonderful, both the male cadets I worked with during the day and the mostly female graduate students in the evenings. Much to my surprise, I even enjoyed the novelty of wearing a uniform and being a part of all the pomp and tradition. I even felt disappointed I couldn't carry a sword. But the oppression was truly smothering, taking the form of a rigidity among many of my colleagues that was frustrating for students just as it was uncomfortable for me.

Chief among my complaints was that the predecessor in my position was determined to run me out of there as fast as he could. I tried to not take it all that personally, since I was hardly the first to be a victim of his wrath and certainly would not be the last. Unfortunately, I have never "done" transference all that well with my own clients, much less with others who have acted out toward me.

We therapists, you see, are supposed to be experts at not taking things personally when other people are projecting "their stuff" onto us. I do know all the right moves and fake them quite well. I tell myself, over and over again, "He is not really mad at me. He doesn't even really know me. I just push his buttons, and he is trying to protect himself."

Repeating this mantra of comfort works fairly well when I am in session with a client. It lets me off the hook just long enough to figure out whether I really have done something deserving of such a vehement response. Since most of the time the other person really is transferring unresolved issues onto me, it's a good thing that I'm so good at pretending I am not the least perturbed by the force of anger directed my way. No doubt you have noticed that "pretend" is the operative word here. I *do* feel bothered by these interactions, far more than I let anyone know.

In spite of the discomfort I felt being part of an organization that espoused some values I had always opposed and among colleagues who had different notions about the way the program should be run, I loved being in the classroom full-time once again. If I hadn't received a phone call from a friend at the University of Nevada, Las Vegas, inviting me to apply for a position, I might still be in Charleston.

Nah. But I might have stayed a little longer.

Life in the Desert

When the department chair called to invite me to an interview, I thought of it as a free trip to Vegas, no strings attached. The only thing that I knew about the University of Nevada, Las Vegas, was that it had an amazing basketball team and that it was located by The Strip. While these weren't exactly selling points for me, I also found out that the place had oodles of resources and was growing like crazy. Moreover, I was not prepared for how hungry I felt for professional companionship. Here was a department of seventeen professionals (count them—seventeen other educators who do what I do) who seemed bright and energetic. Furthermore, in keeping with the image of the laid back West, some of them were actually wearing blue jeans and sandals to class. Coming from a place where I had to wear a military uniform, I found this mighty impressive.

So I am now, finally, a lucky man. Sometimes it takes a number of attempts in order to get what we really want. Rather than being discouraged, each time I have faced a working environment that does not provide the kind of support I want, I have looked elsewhere. I have been in enough places to know that petty politics, power struggles, bureaucratic insensitivity, incompetent and manipulative supervisors, interpersonal conflicts and coalitional battles are everywhere. That is certainly no exception in my present situation. The difference now is that the large staff affords me some choices about whom I want to be around.

During my tenure and promotion process, for example, there were a few people who attempted to sabotage me. One among them was willing to resort to almost any lengths to orchestrate my demise. Part of my growth as a therapist is that I can now exercise greater restraint in the actions I take in response to disappointment or disillusionment. In previous years I have been inclined to withdraw, then to run away. Fortunately, I have always been able to create these other options for myself. This time, however, I felt part of a group of colleagues who, even if they don't understand me, work pretty hard to be supportive. I am around people whom I can talk to daily about my work, who are as open to learning from me as I am from them. This is my way out of the dark. I no longer feel so alone.

I was, at first, perplexed as to how these close relationships with a half dozen colleagues developed so quickly. Trust among grown-up adults, especially in a competitive academic environment, is not very forthcoming. However, we had a common enemy, a feeling of being under bombardment by hostile forces, and that pulled us together. There is nothing like an outside threat to bring people together.

Practicing What We Preach

During these past decades, as I have worked in the company of other therapists and educators, I have continued to be concerned about not only my own hypocrisy in not always practicing what I preach but also that of my colleagues. I have been amazed at how insensitive, power hungry, manipulative, and unscrupulous some of my colleagues have been. Aren't we supposed to be models for our students? Aren't we supposed to demonstrate in our own lives that which we ask of them?

I guess not. I have had the misfortune to be associated with a number of colleagues, both therapists and educators, who were primarily attracted to this field out of a desire to manipulate and control others. If that is your personal goal, just imagine how dangerous you could be in exploiting or hurting others who are in a one-down position when you have had years of training in how to read what others are thinking, how to identify their areas of vulnerability, and how to get them to do things they would rather not.

You can also imagine the sometimes comic, sometimes tragic consequences of putting eighteen professors in a room together and trying to get us to agree on anything. We are all used to getting our way, to having people in our classrooms show us deference and even reverence. We are each convinced that our particular opinion is right and everyone else's is clearly out of line. Perhaps you think this is no different than the situation in any organization in which there are many educated, ambitious professionals. What is unique, however, is that we are supposedly teaching beginners to the field about compassion and empathy and kindness. I have been absolutely amazed how little these values and qualities are evident in the behavior of those I have worked with.

What do I say to a student who comes into my office crying because another professor screamed at her for not doing things the way he preferred? What do I tell others who wonder aloud how another professor can teach them anything when he is personally ineffective in his own life? And most of all, how can I feel good about the work I am doing, trying to inspire people to be loving and caring, when there are others around me who are systematically collecting trophies of pain? One among them has been known to brag that he has made every female member of our department, faculty and secretaries alike, break into tears.

The reality I have come to understand is that every university, and every corporation or other group of people, has a few people who are competent and kind and a few who are less so. If every time I encounter such unscrupulous or unsympathetic colleagues, I move on to somewhere else, I will only end up punishing myself, not to mention my students, in the process.

I have grown over time to be a bit less sensitive to other people's meanness. I am working harder to immunize myself against others who don't care for me or respect what I do. I am still trying to look at what it is within me that invites these occasional conflicts with others, while I am learning to recognize that I am no more exempt than anyone else.

It is sensitivity to and trust of others that allows me to be most effective in my roles as teacher and therapist. Yet it is these same characteristics that make me most vulnerable to being hurt and prone to overreacting to circumstances in which others don't respond the way I would prefer. As a therapist, I have helped many people deal with these identical struggles. It is with the support of my current colleagues that I am finally making significant progress with myself in these same areas.

Globe Trotting

If I am going to stick around for a while, to stifle my wanderlust at least until my son graduates from high school, I have to find a way to move on and yet stay in the same place. If I am also to recognize that no matter where I go some people will not like me as much as I prefer, I damn well better grow up and live with that reality.

The compromise that I have worked out for myself is never to teach summers in the desert. I take that time not so much to recover from the stresses and strains of the academic year as to practice my craft elsewhere for a limited stint. I make plans, sometimes years in advance, to find an exchange, a grant, or a visiting lectureship that will give me a taste of another life without my having to make a permanent move. A perfect arrangement, I marvel, for someone striving for perfection.

I discovered this arrangement quite by accident after I stumbled into an opportunity to live and work in Singapore and Malaysia for a summer, all expenses paid by a government grant. Although my schedule was grueling and the assignment not what I would have preferred, who can argue with an opportunity to live in Southeast Asia? On the plane home, I was already planning how I might repeat this scenario the following year. I arranged a lecture tour in New Zealand, another place I had always wanted to visit. Traveling with my family part of the time and on my own for a month, I spoke to groups in all parts of the country—from bustling cities to isolated outposts. Enamored by the culture, the people, and the way a teacher works in that country, I returned the following summer for a more protracted stay in a single location, experiencing an alternative life, being another person in a faraway land.

After each of these summer adventures, I return invigorated and refreshed. Tempered now by experiences working with Malaysian, Chinese, Maori, or Bantu people, my perspective on what I do as a teacher and therapist has expanded exponentially. I can not only compare what it's like to be a teacher in New Zealand, Tanzania, Borneo, and North Alabama, but I know in my gut what is universal about helping people to find their way.

Between the legends and the lies I have created for myself in my life is the realization that my struggle to come to terms with my need to be appreciated is what has driven me so hard to be a perfect teacher. The legend I tell myself is that I have made my choices in order to help a greater number of others; the lie is that I strive to be a perfect teacher to heal myself. Yet no matter how hard I try and how carefully I work, I remember not so much what I have done to make a difference as what I should have done to have had an even greater impact.

17

What I Should Have Done

O ne of the problems with teaching therapy and writing books
on the subject is that I now understand all too well the way
things are supposed to be. I study videotapes of sessions the way intel-
ligence agents scour satellite photos. During any single supervision
session, I can point out hundreds of things a therapist might have
done differently. Simultaneously, I attend to body language, non-
verbal communication, voice intonation, choice of language, surface and deep communication, and interventions selected and
executed. There are a dozen major therapeutic skills to be evaluated
in terms of their effectiveness according to a number of scales. Then
there is that "felt sense," or intuition, that something is not going
quite right.

When I compare what I do in any given therapy or class session
to what someone else might do, or what I would have done if I
could do it again, I sometimes feel my work is futile. I am haunted
by my mistakes and misjudgments. When I take the role of practitioner, several times in every session I kick myself for something
incredibly stupid or insensitive I have said. The client hardly notices
and just continues on with a monologue, while I sit there, momentarily distracted, berating myself for incompetence. Since I teach
therapy to others, I am supposed to understand better than most
what should be done in any situation.

The problem is compounded by the reality that at any given

moment there are an infinite number of reasonable things that a clinician might do. If ten practitioners heard a client say, "My mother made me do it," it is conceivable that they could have many different legitimate responses. The mental activity that takes place in those few seconds before one must respond may be furious:

> Should I attend to his belief in external control, that his actions are not within his own power? Maybe I should reflect his underlying feelings of helplessness. Better yet, I could ask him to describe more fully his experience. Or maybe I should find out a bit more about his relationship with his mother. I could also check out how this pattern is recurring in his life. I wonder if I might be better off moving into an action mode by asking him to describe the way he would like things to be. It's probably better to ignore the whole topic and ask him to elaborate more on what he was discussing earlier. Or perhaps I should say nothing at all and just let him continue.

What is truly incredible is that, whatever option is chosen, upon reflection there is every reason to believe that there are several other interventions that would have been far preferable. These are not just the obsessive ruminations of a perfectionist; we become better in our craft by considering ways that we might do things differently in the future. That is what I attempt to teach my students.

Ultimately, I believe that the choice of intervention and the execution of skill is relatively unimportant, at least within certain parameters. In other words, as long as a clinician abides by some basic rules of customary conduct (not to be exploitive, to encourage self-responsibility, to be respectful, and so on), it probably does not matter as much what we do as who we are. That is why therapists who appear to operate in divergent ways can all be effective— they are not as different as they think. It does not matter so much whether they confront, interpret, summarize, or reflect, whether they execute their skills perfectly or not. Clients give us the benefit of the doubt when they can feel our caring.

Do I really believe this if I am so concerned with the supposed mistakes that I make? Actually, I only half-subscribe to the notion that presence is what matters most. The other half of what counts, and it is just as crucial, is that there are better choices that can be made, given the unique client, situation, and presenting issues. I am only aware afterwards that something I said or did was probably not all that helpful and maybe even harmful. I wish I could take it back. I forgive myself as best I can and move on to something else. If I have done my job of being as compassionate and responsive as I am able, then clients also forgive the mistakes. They may even like me more for being imperfectly human.

If it is who we are that matters most, then who am I? I would hope that in my teaching as well as in my clinical work I come across as someone who is cheerfully flawed. Yet I hope that it is equally evident that I am working fairly hard to improve myself.

It is the drive to do better that is partially responsible for what I believe is a standard of excellence in my work. Each semester I review the student evaluations of my teaching. Since I am sensitive and responsive, since I put so much of myself into my classes, the results of these assessments are quite impressive, among the most favorable in the college. In a class of thirty students, typically fifteen will think I am the best instructor they have ever had; another ten will view the class as excellent; three others will rate it as fair; and the last two will hate my guts and find the class to be a waste of time.

My reaction to these data is quite revealing. I skim the averages that show evaluations of 4.8 on a 5.0 scale, and feel quite satisfied for a few moments. Then I immediately look at the comments of the students who did not like me. All the while I tell myself that, no matter who I am and what I do, there will be a few people who don't care for me, I still focus unduly on those few. Where did I go wrong? What could I have done differently? Is there some merit to their criticism? I mentally replay conversations from the class, at first to disqualify their feedback as the rumblings of those who feel threatened. There was a point early in my career when this was all I was willing to do—simply write these people off as bitter or defensive. I try now to give them the benefit of the doubt. I assume that what they have to offer me, even if it may be from a distorted perspective, does have the seeds of some worthwhile message.

A similar internal process takes place when I am doing therapy as well. I used to disown failure by writing off the disenfranchised: they have some ax to grind, they don't want to succeed, they are too threatened to change, they would be critical of anything, they would be tough for anyone to deal with. This strategy works quite well if the object is to escape acknowledging one's own imperfections. I must like this acknowledgment, however, because I look for opportunities to do it every chance I get. Obviously, I put a lot of pressure on myself. The result, or so I tell myself, is a higher standard of excellence.

Perhaps the single most frequent problem that I have had in relationships throughout my life is that friends and colleagues have assumed that I hold the same standards for them that I do for myself. When I have collaborated on projects, workshops, or books, I make my partners nervous. I appear fluid and graceful when I do these things. To the outsider, it looks like they are easy for me. People don't realize how hard I work at this, how many sleepless nights I sit around writing in my journal or just talking to myself, planning out what I want to do and how I want to do it.

It does seem true that others with whom I have worked seem to struggle more to express themselves the way they would like. When they compare their way of working to mine, a decidedly informal and personal style, differences between us become heightened. I must not communicate enough to them about what I am thinking and feeling, for often their assumption is that I am judging them, and doing so quite harshly. I hear that comment sometimes from clients and students as well. And each time, I search deep inside for evidence that I am judging them, and I come up empty.

Maybe this is my dark side. Perhaps I really am more judgmental than I pretend, even to myself. I have been told that I don't show much on my face when I am listening, that only when I finally speak does the student, client, or colleague feel reassured that I am truly with them. Still, I don't feel, on the inside, all that critical of the different ways others may do things. Yet I would only have to reread my own words in the previous chapter to find that I do indeed have some strong opinions about how others should be just like me.

Oh, my gosh, how I hate admitting this! I suppose what I am realizing is that to continue my growth in this area I will have to practice what I preach more often. Although I advertise myself as being accepting and forgiving and tolerant of styles different from my own, in fact I am as demanding as many of those with whom I am in disagreement—a classic case of projection in which I disown those parts of me that are most unacceptable.

If one part that I would prefer to leave alone is the secret self that is critical of others' being different, the other part I would prefer to leave alone is the hidden self that wants to hurt them for being different. Inside, I do my best to keep my hostility, anger, and aggression under wraps. I don't do anger. When I feel it, I pretend I don't. When I show anger, I try to disguise it, dilute it, deny its existence.

Anger is synonymous for me with being out of control. It is often abusive of other people, but just as significantly, it feels like the ultimate in self-abuse. Since I do not allow myself the option of being angry, or at least of expressing anger explicitly, others must sense my contempt or disapproval. Since they cannot be certain when I am being judgmental, they must imagine, in spite of my claims to the contrary, that I am feeling disdainful even when that is the furthest thing from my mind.

If the truth be told (and that is the purpose of this book), I am overly preoccupied with what I should have done—as a teacher, a therapist, and a human being. Likewise, I spend more time than I let on thinking critically about how others are behaving. Even though I deny these hostile judgments (even when confronted directly), they are a primary means by which I skate through life feeling better than everyone else. Yet, lest I begin to take myself too seriously, this feeling of specialness is balanced by an even more dominant core judgment—that no matter how hard I try and what I do, I will always be found wanting.

18

Found Wanting

I have just received a memo announcing that meetings have been scheduled to evaluate me for tenure and promotion at the institution in which I am currently employed. I have been through this before, several times actually, but each time I have moved onward it has been with the understanding that my new colleagues will have to decide all over again whether I am worthy enough to remain among them. As much as I dread this process, I must not find it so abhorrent that I am unwilling to put myself on the line and start over again.

Rationally, I tell myself many of the same things I tell clients and students: "People can evaluate your performance but *never* the essence of who you are," or, "You have done everything that you can; the rest is outside of your control," or, "*You* know how hard you have worked; what difference does it make what others think?" or, "Even if they don't evaluate you favorably, that does not mean the end of the world, just a minor setback."

The truth of the matter is that I don't believe these rationalizations for more than a few moments. I can remind myself over and over again that nobody could do as much as I have done, no one is more dedicated or highly motivated, nor has anyone been as productive. How many books must I write, people must I impress, or accomplishments must I catalogue before I have proven, once and for all, that I am finally good enough? The answer is that there will never be enough. I will always be found wanting.

I could be awarded tenure or promotion unanimously by my peers, and my elation would last only as long as it would take the whispers to begin inside my head: "It happened only because they were being nice," or, "Their standards weren't all that high to begin with," or most believable of all, "I fooled them again." I am simply a fine actor who pretends to be competent; I am so good at acting that almost everyone thinks that I really do know what I am doing. Those few colleagues who did question the value of what I have accomplished in my career saw through me. They know I can be found wanting.

I read reviews of my books that are mostly quite complimentary; many are even quite enthusiastic in their praise. I fooled the reviewers too. I ignore their support for my work and zero in on the paragraph that mentions some weakness they have found. Even through my defensiveness and hurt (which I work hard to hide), I acknowledge they have pegged me accurately. Yes, I could have done more. If only I were a little brighter, more thorough and patient, more perceptive and creative, then I could have produced something quite valuable instead of this contribution to mediocrity.

Of course, I realize that I take all of this too personally. I tell interns every day that there are limits to what they can do. I understand that some people will dislike me no matter what I do or who I am. I know that there are some people who have lousy attitudes that contribute far more to their reactions to me than anything that I do. But I wonder: do I really *know* these things if I am always found wanting? What does it mean that I appear to so many others as a mentor, as an ideal model of what they would like to be, when I feel so flawed inside? What will people do when they find out the truth? Will they throw down this book in disgust?

I think about what it would take in order for me no longer to be found wanting. Well, education didn't help. The more degrees I accumulated, the higher I set my standards. Therapy works for a lit-

tle while, but then either the effects wear off or, more likely, I figure out how to circumvent some of the benefits through persistent
countermeasures. Achievement is a nifty little trap: the more I
accomplish, the better I feel about myself and the more I think I
must be all right; then I feel even more dishonest about pretending
to know things that I do not.

When I ask other people about this phenomenon, most admit to
feeling quite similar. Even the most confident among us are harbor-
ing secret doubts about their sense of competence. Deep down inside,
I am convinced that almost all individuals are found wanting—by
those who know them best, by strangers who form first impressions,
and most of all, by their own secret admission. No one is sufficiently
attentive, patient, responsive, understanding, sensitive, or attractive.
Everyone is too stubborn or compliant, passive or aggressive, ambitious or lazy, opinionated or wimpy. We don't begin to satisfy other
people's demands and expectations, much less our own. Found wanting, we slither through life hoping that people won't notice, or if
they do, that we can somehow convince them to keep quiet.

If only I could stay quiet, then I wouldn't bring so much attention to my own inadequacies. People are hardly aware of my failings; they are too busy monitoring their own. I mentioned
previously that in the early days when I was first learning to be a
therapist, detailed self-scrutiny was the norm. Every session was
recorded on videotape, every word, gesture, and pimple was available for later analysis by my supervisor, whose stated job was to find
fault with my performance. In no time at all, I became all too aware
of everything I did wrong in a session. I was too earnest; I should
lighten up a bit. My reflections of feelings were shallow and lacked
the ring of authenticity. My posture was wooden; I appeared nervous (I *was* nervous). My interpretations missed the mark. My con-
frontations were premature. My stories were long-winded; my
self-disclosures were too indulgent. Other than that, I didn't kill
anyone, and I and my client both survived, so the session wasn't too
bad after all.

I internalized this critical voice. I imagined that for the rest of my professional life, every time I bungled an intervention in my office or offered a low-level response in the classroom, the client or student would immediately cry out, "Now *that* was awfully stupid. You say that you are a *professional?*" For months afterward, every time I made some mistake or misjudgment (about once every three minutes, and that was if I kept my mouth shut), I was amazed to discover that not only did clients and students not say anything to me when I was inept, but they didn't even notice! They were so engrossed in their own failings, so concerned with explaining to me why I should like them even though they were flawed, that they were not the least aware that I was doing much the same thing.

When I am teaching newcomers to the field in their first practical experiences, I am reminded all over again of the ways I would operate inside my head as I was trying to be helpful to someone else. I have found it amusing, if not instructive to my students, to imagine the kinds of internal conversational dialogues going on inside the client and me at the same time:

Client: And so I told her she shouldn't do that. *[Am I whining? I know I must sound like a real loser.]* I tried real hard to stand up for myself. *[I wish I didn't let people get to me like this.]*

Me: I'm not sure if you are trying to convince me or yourself. *[Huh? Where am I going with that one? I hope he doesn't ask me to explain.]*

Client: What do you mean? *[If only I was smarter I would know what he is referring to. Now he will really think I'm a dolt. He probably already explained this once, and I forgot.]*

Me: I only meant to *[do I sound defensive?]* point out that you do tend to spend a lot of time trying to explain *["justify" would have been better]* why you don't do the things that you want to do. *[Yeah, as if I don't do the same. I wonder if he will challenge me on that?]*

Client: You're right. *[I am hopeless. Why does he even bother with me? He probably only sees me because he feels sorry for me.]*

Me: *[Okay. So what am I supposed to do now? Should I change the sub-*

ject or stay with this? Maybe I should just wait a while. See what he does.]
Yes. *[Now, that was really intelligent. If I were him I'd leave now.]*
Client: Um. *[He's waiting for me to say something. What should I say?]*
Uh. Well, yeah. I was saying you are right *[I already said that. I'm
lost. Help!]*
Me: *[Damn, I lost him! He's waiting for me to bail him out. I have no
idea what to do now. When in doubt, keep the ball in his court.]* Perhaps
it would be better to move on to something else. *[Now he knows for
sure how lost I am.]*
Client: Sure. I agree. *[So now what do I do?]* Well, I was just thinking
about *[I'm lying. Will he catch me?]* what you said earlier, about some
of the other relationships I've struggled through in my life.
Me: Go on. *[I have no idea what he is talking about. Did I say that?]*

And so continues this agonizing exercise in self-doubt and self-
berating. The miracle is how often even dialogues like this are therapeutic for the client and even for the therapist. As I listen to my
students talk about how insecure they are, I feel much better. I feel
guilty about feeling better. I am supposed to be in a compassionate
frame of mind, one in which I am positively radiating empathetic
energy. But I can't help but gloat a little inside: "And I thought
that *I* was messed up. I guess I am better off than I thought. Look
at *this* guy!"

I have even heard it said by more than a few practitioners that
the reason they joined this exclusive club is so they could be around
others who are worse off than they are. We don't talk about this
much within ourselves, much less among ourselves, but I suspect
this feeling is somewhat universal. I *do* feel better about myself on
those days when I do a lot of teaching and therapy. I am continually reminded that I know things that others apparently do not, that
I can do quite easily things that seem out of reach for others. I may
be wanting, but there are quite a few other folks walking around
who are a lot worse off than I am.

Now this is a heck of a thing for a guy who helps people for a living to say! Okay. I take it all back. I didn't mean it. I was only kidding. Not. So why don't I erase this stuff altogether, move on to something that showcases me as the hero I wish to be? Why do I persist in airing out those parts of me that I despise the most?

This is my journey toward self-acceptance. If I can come to terms with the ugliest, smelliest, most vile parts of me, and admit them out loud for all to hear (or read), there will be nothing left for me to hide. I will have beaten you to the punch. You won't be able to hurt me anymore because I will have already raked myself over the coals.

I find myself wishing we all would do this more. There is no doubt that the more honest and forthcoming people are about their foibles and failings the more I like them. I know that is the most seductive part of me as well. People at professional conferences want to touch the vulnerability that they have only heard or read about. Maybe it makes them feel better to know that someone who is supposedly so well-known is more messed up than they are. Maybe they are attracted to frankness for its own sake, no matter how self-deprecating. Perhaps there is comfort in finding out that someone who is supposedly knowledgeable can be found wanting, a quite ordinary fellow after all.

19

Sharing What I Know

It is frustrating being a therapist. Sometimes I feel as if I have said the most brilliant, witty things in a session; I look at my client, and it's obvious that she didn't understand a word that was said. She is in her own world. Then I shrug because the wisdom was lost. Even I don't remember what I said that seemed so significant at the time.

Each session is like a painted canvas, or at the least, a signed lithograph. I create a masterpiece every hour for a world that has but two ears. Although having an audience of one is certainly better than talking to myself, it does not have nearly the kick that comes with reaching an audience of several dozen in a classroom, tens of thousands in an article or book, hundreds of thousands in a television appearance.

There are many instances when therapists invent some new way of looking at the world, create some wonderful metaphor, or describe a complicated idea in accessible terms, then realize they were speaking to an audience of one. Therapists cannot help but feel unappreciated, especially when they realize that often they are working harder than their clients. Some of the most brilliant, profound thoughts ever uttered on this planet have fallen on deaf ears in a therapist's chambers.

I think about some of the people I have worked with. Ron is a lonely, melancholic fellow who spends his time weight lifting and masturbating. At thirty-five, he has never kissed a girl and is para-lyzed at the prospect of any social interaction. I have seen him weekly for almost a year, and I am not sure that I can detect any-thing about him that is different. Each week, he skulks into the office, always at dusk when the lighting is dim, making him appear even more forlorn. His eyes are downcast, hands clenched, feet shuf-fling. Although he nods attentively, I am not certain that he has heard a single word I have said to him in the fifty weeks we have spent together. If he has heard, he sure has not acted on what was said. I am working far harder than he is, and I seem to be more upset with the direction his empty life is headed.

There are names we give to people like Ron, labels that seem to imply he has some rare disease that is intractable and incurable. It certainly seems that way sometimes to those of us who try to make contact. Whatever we say or ask them to do, such clients seem inca-pable of following through.

Even the best-adjusted folks who come for help feel ambivalent about what they are asked to do. Certainly, they want to improve the quality of their lives but not if it involves much pain or work. They have their own agendas; much of the time, they don't even want to hear what I have to offer. It is too threatening. If they lis-ten, if they agree with the ideas that are offered, they will have to make dramatic changes to realign their thinking and action. It is far easier to tune out what is said. Nod your head and pretend you are listening. Say, "uh huh." Then change the subject.

Teaching is a different story altogether. In the classroom, not only can I make lots of people listen to me, but I can make them actually take notes and even test them to make sure they heard me. What incredible power! What a rush! Even if a third of the students are daydreaming and another third are resisting and warding off the ideas presented, that still leaves a full third who are being influenced. Sometimes even a single soul who really understands is enough.

I truly come alive when I am in the classroom. I love the atten-tion, the power, the incredible exhilaration of making someone laugh or helping someone to understand something that had previously been out of reach. I can actually see the light go on behind people's eyes when something strikes home, especially an idea that will change their lives forever. That is the kick of teaching this stuff. We are not talking about quantum mechanics here, but subjects that have immediate application to life—improving relationships and communication skills: being more self-analytic, changing aspects of yourself that are dysfunctional.

In a single class session, I can teach people how to change forever the way they relate to others, and to themselves. Sometimes this growth takes place literally before my eyes. I see a budding teacher or counselor struggling to make contact with an assigned partner. I make a few corrections, suggest a different way of listening and talking, and then, wow! a dramatically different result. Then people take these skills home. They apply them with their own children, parents, spouses, and friends and notice how much more intimacy they can create in their lives.

I love the moment when I *know* I have students in the palm of my hands. Like the comedian or entertainer who feels his responsive audience, I find teaching an exercise in rapture. I am saying things I have never said before, in a way that is reaching others. My whole body vibrates; my soul radiates excitement and enthusiasm. I want students to feel they are so special that this and every moment have been created just for them. That's why I refuse to teach the same thing the same way over and over. I have taught the topic of group therapy about a hundred times in courses or workshops, and those sessions have never been the same. Each semester, I learn new things about how groups operate and how to teach people about those principles.

I have narcissistic reasons why teaching eclipses my dark side. If truth be told, I absolutely love the control I feel when I am in front of a class. There is nowhere else where I get to decide what we do and how long we do it. If I am bored, we get to do something else. If I want to take a break or end class early or keep students late, that is my prerogative. In spite of the pains I take to present myself as flexible, tolerant, permissive, forgiving, and accepting, there is an unstated understanding that I am in charge. If a student speaks at the same time I do, I win. If I don't wish to answer a question or deal with an issue, I can deftly change the subject. If I don't like something that someone is doing, I can force her to stop. If I want to tell a story that is only tangentially related to the subject at hand, I can indulge myself. If I was inclined to inspire fear or anxiety, I could do that as well.

Where else in the world can I get away with this power and freedom? In other settings of my life, I am not listened to more than anyone else. I have to fight to be heard. My family and friends may find me endearing or intelligent, but they still don't listen to me any more than to anyone else. That is only fair.

One of the things that I and others who are college professors and authors tend to do is take ourselves too seriously. We forget that once out of our classrooms we are no more important than anyone else. Few people care what we think once we lose the authority to assign grades on their performance. We are seen as pompous, arrogant, or perhaps benignly eccentric. Moreover, writing and counseling are lonely businesses; rarely do I get the kind of feedback I want to know if I am making contact. How do I know that you, the reader, are not scowling or shaking your head in disgust this very moment? And without such information, I have no way of knowing whether I am reaching you, whether we are in sync. I have no opportunity to change course, to elaborate on the parts you find most interesting, or to stay away from the areas that are not useful to you.

In therapy, at least, I am able to track the effects of what I do, to note the impact of interventions on the client. But it is teaching that really infuses me with power. There is nothing like an audience for sheer overload of input. At any given moment, I can see a dozen different faces reacting to what I am doing. I can witness the effects of my words and actions not just on a single subject but on a whole group of folks. Even more exciting, there are interactive effects as people speak and react to one another. I see eyes making contact across the room, furtive whispers to the left and right, a note being hurriedly scribbled to a friend. I can tell who is attracted to another, and who holds another in disdain. I see the coalitions in the group as clearly as if they were visibly labeled. The classroom environment is incredibly rich and active. And there I am, in the middle of it all, making much of it happen.

If I can't die in bed or skiing down a powdery slope, then I hope I keel over in the middle of a class.

Part VII

Confident Helper

20

· ·

Your Zipper Is Open

I was sitting at a lunch meeting with a dozen other people I had never met before. Across from me was a woman contentedly munching on her salad, oblivious to the dab of creamy garlic dressing that was resting on her nose. It was fairly obvious that others had noticed she was wearing part of her meal, but nobody said anything. I discretely signalled for her attention, and then pointed to my nose with a napkin. She gratefully wiped the smudge away.

At first, I wondered if I had been presumptuous. After all, I didn't even know this person. What did books of etiquette say about this sort of thing? Then it occurred to me that what I do for a living is tell people they have smudges on their noses, their zippers are open, or their behavior might not be in their best interests. I am paid to speak the truth, to say things to people that nobody else has the courage or inclination to say.

Many people go through life doing things that are profoundly irritating to others. They have speech habits or mannerisms that put others off. They do things that block the likelihood that they will get what they want. They unknowingly rub others the wrong way or recruit losers into their lives, unaware of their repeated mistakes. And who will tell them? Will you? When was the last time somebody gave you honest feedback on how you are perceived?

Apart from anything else that I do—presenting information

concisely, explaining ideas in ways that they become more comprehensible, clarifying what others are thinking and feeling, motivating people to try new strategies, providing support as it is needed—I try my hardest to tell people when their behavior appears self-defeating.

I observe a student rambling on about a time in her life when she lived someplace else and did something or other. Nobody is listening. She doesn't notice. I interrupt her and ask where she is going. What point is she making? After stumbling around for another few minutes, she eventually admits she doesn't know what she is trying to say. I tell her that just as others in this class tune her out when she speaks, so must other people in her life. How does this fit for her? She nods her head once, twice, looks away and whispers that she needs help.

I am supervising a therapist who is eager to please, so much so that I can't recall a single instance when he ever disagreed with me about anything. I check this out with him. After all these hours we have spent together, how come he has never challenged anything that I have ever offered to him? Naturally, he agrees with this observation as well, but cannot think of anything I ever said that he might object to. When I follow this up with a question about whom he does feel he can safely disagree with, he can't think of anyone. "Conflict is just not my style," he adds defensively. When I ask him what the consequences are of being so compliant, he admits that not only in his personal life but also with his clients he may be cheating others of valuable opportunities for more intimate and honest engagement.

A client ends almost every statement she makes with the question "Do you know what I mean?" I ask her if she is used to not being understood, given that she requires such explicit reassurance that her messages have been received. We talk about the uncertainty and insecurity she communicates by this style of relating to others. Nobody has ever mentioned this to her before, but she now sees why she is often not taken very seriously.

Finally, a colleague protests to me that he does not covet a particular position that has become available. It would be too much work and aggravation, not worth the sacrifices he would have to make. "Liar!" I tell him. He looks stunned, demands that I explain what I mean. I reply softly and carefully, "It is just that while you say you don't want this job, I sense that you really do want the challenge. Something is holding you back from going after what you want."

In each of these cases, and a thousand others that I can think of, my primary job was one of telling people things they needed to hear but were unlikely to be told by others. I have thus trained myself to attend to personal and interpersonal functioning with a critical eye: How might she do that differently? What is it about his style that diminishes what he is saying? Is she aware of the effect she has on others? How could his approach be fine-tuned to be more effective? Does he know that he has a zipper, much less that it is open?

None of the examples I just described are beyond the scope of what most any therapist can do. The difference might be that I try very hard to carry forth this frankness from the therapeutic arena into all facets of my life. Of course, many people do not care to know they have garlic dressing on their noses, toilet paper on the bottoms of their shoes, or that their zippers are open. At least, they would rather discover these oversights on their own instead of having them pointed out by me.

There seems to be some tremendous shame in being confronted with our imperfections, as if we were caught doing something that we should not have been. It is all right to make mistakes, but don't allow anyone else to notice. If you are caught red-handed, deny it, and if that doesn't work, blame somebody else.

I am so grateful when someone takes the time and makes the investment to help me face something I am doing that is less than self-enhancing. Of course, I have to be convinced that this person is operating from a stance of love and care rather than trying to hurt me in some way. If there is some doubt, if I wonder if this person has a hidden agenda, if he or she might be trying to gain some advantage by putting me down, then my mistrust overpowers everything else. Under such circumstances, if I even hear what is being said, I am doing my best to disqualify the speaker or invalidate the message.

A colleague points out to me that some action I took was ill-advised. I immediately become defensive, firing off a salvo of reasons why he is misinformed and why he misperceived what took place. During the process of reloading, I marvel at what is going on within me, how important it is that I don't acknowledge fault in any way. Rather than feeling grateful for his advice, I feel pinned to the wall. This is hardly surprising I realize—I do not trust this man nor do I believe he is really trying to help me; on the contrary, I believe he is putting me down.

Another colleague suggests that the next time I am faced with a particular situation I might respond a bit differently than I have in the past. He proceeds to point out what specific things I did, what impact they may have had on others, and what alternatives might produce different results. I hug him impulsively, filled with gratitude for his time, effort, and caring in reaching out to me. Not only do I hear quite clearly what he is saying, but I know immediately how I can act differently in the future. This man has, in some small way, changed my life for the better. What a gift he has offered me!

The difference between these two examples is that in the latter case, I am certain that the man is trying to help me. I don't wonder about his motives because I trust him. In the first instance, however, previous experiences have led me to question the person's intentions—I neither trust him, nor particularly value anything that he might offer. He could tell me that my zipper was open, and I would immediately think, "Damn it! Why did *he* have to see that?"

It is not enough to see and hear clearly. It is not enough to recognize that someone else is doing something self-defeating. The last part is equally important: you must to be able to tell someone about it in a way that he or she can hear without feeling defensive. I suppose that is another reason (besides my effort at self-healing) I am writing this book—in the hope that maybe, in some way, I can tell you that you have garlic dressing on your nose, or that your zipper is open, and in so doing, alter your life forever. I have discovered that the least threatening way to do that is by revealing myself to you as honestly as I possibly can. Maybe then you will trust my intentions. Perhaps then you may be willing to look at yourself.

21

One Hundred Lives

Another therapist once remarked about me to a client I was seeing, "I don't know about that guy—he moves around a lot." Left unstated was the judgment that perhaps I was either looking for something I could not find or fleeing from something that was getting closer. In either case, the message was that I was somehow suspect, unstable, or unsavory because I did not stay in one place for very long. I have wondered what kind of role model I am for my clients and students, leading the life of a gypsy, packing up and moving my family every few years. What is wrong with me that I can't sink roots and establish myself as a permanent part of one place or another?

My reputation is well deserved. I do become bored easily with routines. I do feel restless and itchy when I have stayed in one spot for more than a few years. I always wonder what life might be like somewhere else. When I was a child and first learned about a creature called a genie, who granted wishes after one rubbed his lamp, I gave up my fantasy of trying to fly like Superman. After donning a towel as a make-believe cape and jumping off couches and chairs, I had eventually came to terms with the idea that I could probably not defy gravity. But a magic lamp? Maybe if I looked long and hard enough, I could find one of those! Or so went my childhood reveries, as I drifted away from whatever was going on in class.

I gave considerable thought to what I would wish for, should I discover such a wondrous object as Aladdin's lamp, and I decided that I would wish for a hundred lives. Since I couldn't quite make the leap of faith that allows one to believe in reincarnation (besides, who would want to come back as a slug?), the next best thing would be, if possible, to strike a bargain for an infinite number of lifetimes (at that time, the number 100 seemed infinite enough).

Well, obviously (I hope), I have grown up a bit since then. I don't believe any longer in genies or the tooth fairy. I have not, however, given up the wish that I could live a hundred lifetimes, even if I have to squeeze them into a handful of decades. I go about living my life with an urgency. Time, and so precious little of it, is all I have. In this brief ride that I have been granted, I want to see and do as much as I can before the old roller coaster comes to an abrupt halt, launching me out into nothingness.

The life-style of a therapist is conducive to this journey of a hundred lives. Every client I see offers me a glimpse into another existence that is beyond my reach. Most people wonder what it might be like to be gay or wealthy, to be a professional athlete or prostitute, to have been born on a reservation, in a refugee camp, or the lap of luxury. Not only do I get to know the most intimate secrets of such people's lives, but again, I can ask questions! I hope that these inquiries are remotely related to the client's presenting complaints, but they need not necessarily be so; most people like to answer personal questions when they have an attentive listener. While I do my best to censor nosy wonderings that are just for my own curiosity or entertainment, it is easy to justify almost any line of inquiry under the guise of getting a feeling for the client's world. Presumably, I need a sense of the client's experience if I ever hope to promote greater self-understanding and articulated changes in that client.

A client walks in who is a Franciscan monk or a Las Vegas showgirl, and I think, "Wow! I've always wondered what that kind of life must be like." As I get to know both people over time, in a way that each claims is the most intimate relationship they have ever had, I experience their lives vicariously. I learn what it is like to walk the streets of the inner city as a source of spiritual support, breaking up fights, providing comfort to lost souls without hope. Many months later, after the monk leaves my care, grateful for the help I have provided, I realize that I will miss him dearly. I liked living through him; no, I *loved* it. I learned what monks do to find reciprocal love. I learned about the inner politics of the Roman Catholic Church. I learned my way around parts of my city that I am too fearful to visit in person.

I lived another life through the dancer as well. What is it like to do the same shows, day after day, for years without a break? What do you see out there when you are on stage? Are you propositioned often? How do you handle that? What do the women talk about backstage when they are getting ready? My questions are endless. I want to know what each life is like. This is more than voyeurism, although I suspect that all therapists have a healthy dose of that. For me, the act of helping is predicated on my being able to enter the client's life, not as an observer but a participant. When the relationship ends, whether in weeks or years, I must move on to other lives, sometimes wistful that I can no longer be a dancer or a monk.

Clients are people on the move. They are in transition. They are questioning every aspect of their lives, making decisions to change forever the patterns they are living. They are taking tremendous risks, testing their own limits, reaching far beyond what they ever imagined possible. In most cases, they are oozing with excitement over what they are initiating. They are in uncharted territory without a map, yet somehow they are finding their way. They are reporting on the new vistas they have seen, the novel experiences they are creating. Am I jealous? You're darn right!

Here I sit in my same old chair. It is Wednesday, so that means I started the day by getting my son ready for school. Twenty-five minutes on the stair climber, fifteen to shower and get dressed, another twenty-five to get to my office and take my seat, where I now contemplate the day that is likely to unfold. There will be a committee meeting, for example, in which we will argue about things that do not matter; not only will no one remember what we did in this meeting a few months from now, but no one will care. And I will wonder, for the eleven thousandth time, what this faculty dispute has to do with helping students learn. And so on through out the day: there will be a class I have taught thirty times before, a conversation with an advisee that I have had with a hundred preceding students, and a memo to write that nobody will read.

In the meeting, all I can think about is the client I saw yesterday who is experimenting with lesbian love. What would it be like to be gay, I wonder. I am both repelled and intrigued at the same time. The sexual act itself does not seem all that appealing, but the life-style seems interesting. Most of the friends/acquaintances/clients I have known who were gay shared values more similar to my own than the values of any other single group I can think of. So if I were gay. . . . Oops. Somebody in this meeting is talking to me. He expects an answer. Can I tell him where I have been, that I have been living another life?

It is not that what I am currently doing is uninspiring or uninteresting. I cannot think of a time when I have felt more fulfilled, more productive, more energized. I have been working, however, in the same place for over three years. Honestly, I don't see how anyone can do anything for more than a few years without feeling he or she is essentially living the same life over and over again. Not me. Fifty lives down, fifty to go.

22

What Has Moved Me

For any therapist or teacher, it is clients who are both the source of the greatest stress and frustration and the vehicle for personal salvation. I know this is true in my case: I am haunted by images of both hatefulness and unremitting love; by vicious, violent anger and tenderness; by tears of despair and cries of exaltation. Clients and students have moved me in all these ways, for better or worse.

I feel most alive when I am moved—by the stillness of a desert sunset, by the giggles of children playing, by the efforts of people to express their love, and certainly by the lives of those I have been permitted to help. My clients have saved me just as I have saved them. By "save," I don't mean that either they or I have the power to rescue anyone else through force of will; rather that through impact and influence we have *affected* one another in profound ways. We have each been moved by the other's presence.

If I am so fortunate as to have a few minutes of reflection when death looms ahead, I will not be surprised if among the faces I see and voices I hear will be people I tried to help. I have been moved by my clients when even therapists I have hired could not budge me in the same ways. I have learned as much from my clients as I have from any of my teachers. I have felt closer to some of my clients than I have to my most intimate friends. And why not? How many individuals do any of us see regularly in order to talk only about the most private, sacred, and personal aspects of our lives? To whom in our lives do we give complete, undivided attention; total, unconditional acceptance; absolute trust and confidentiality; and unrestrained support and empathy? It is no wonder I feel attached to these folks and they feel beholden to me!

Always a Part of Me

Among the clients who have moved me, "Sasha" has affected me like no other. I suppose this might be because I knew her for such a long time. I first met her when she was a depressed, suicidal teenager, without hope or a future. I sat with her hour after hour, watching her sob helplessly. We did not even talk to one another; I don't think she even looked at me; she just used my office as a place to come and cry.

As I followed her during the next critical years in her life, I watched her grow out of her despair. I would like to think that I was a part of this transformation, although I still don't know what I might have done that made a difference. I know that Sasha trusted me. Totally and completely. I know that she felt safe with me. I know she felt my caring for her, felt that it went beyond mere professional concern and that I cared for her as another person, as a friend. When she hurt, I hurt. When she started to feel no hope, then so did I.

Or perhaps it happened the other way round. Once I started to believe in her, she began believing in herself. No matter. I have not seen her in many years, but my heart is still with her. She is the embodiment of what is possible when one human being sticks by another who is in pain. She will always remind me of what is possible.

Underpaid and Overworked

"Barbie" and "Ken" were hardly a match made in heaven or even in a toy factory. They argued constantly. They bickered. They took turns being the victim and the abuser; each was quite skilled at playing either role. They fought about their children, about money, about sex, about their parents, about their past and their future. I *hate* it when people are mean to one another. I listened to enough of this conflict stuff as I was growing up. My idea of a nightmare is to have to sit in a room alone with two people who take turns trying to hurt one another. Yet I did so for eighty-one consecutive weeks, at $10 an hour.

Strangely, I liked both Barbie and Ken very much. I suppose that is why I wanted so badly for them to get along. And I did everything I could think of to make that happen. I confronted them. I tried to set limits. I got them to try new communication skills. I recorded their conversations and made them listen. I appealed to their concern for their kids. I instituted special rules and restraints. I had them exchange roles. I begged, yelled, pleaded, scolded, argued, pressured, persuaded, and even joined them in the passionate fray. Nothing worked for very long. Each week they returned, carefully placed $10 on my desk, and then launched into their disagreeable battles.

It is now a decade since I have last seen them, and I have no doubt that they are still married. What I eventually realized was that they did just fine the way they were. They did not inflict nearly as much damage on one another with their salvos as they did on me. Once I learned that this was the way that they related to one another, this was how they expressed their love, this was how they "talked" to each other, I stopped seeing their conflict as I normally would. This experience opened up a whole new world for me. Ever since then, I have been able to adapt in a myriad of ways this attitude of recognizing that some people do fine with behaviors that others might consider a problem. In fact, this attitude is the greatest source of my ability to get inside another's experience.

Reliving My Adolescence

When "Meredith" told me on the first day that what she wanted to work on was whether she should have sex or not, and if so, with which guy who is interested in her, I remember rubbing my hands together in glee: finally I would understand how girls think. Meredith was exactly the same age as I was when girls used to tell me that they only liked me "as a friend."

Now here was a fifteen-year-old girl who was actually going through the process of deciding whether to have a sexual experience, and if so, selecting the person she would honor in that way. I can hardly ever recall having more fun with a client, asking her a series of a questions that I had been dying to ask someone her age for a very long time. Why now? What are you looking for exactly? What are the advantages of each of these guys? Are you sure you are ready for this now?

In the process of helping her to realize that perhaps she ought to wait a bit longer before making such an important decision, I also got to relive my own experiences. Meredith was so utterly frank with me, so open and revealing about the way her mind worked, that when we parted company I wanted to thank her for what she taught me. I finally understood what girls of my own era and age were trying to say.

The Power of Belief

"Martha" had so many things wrong with her that I felt like a trauma surgeon trying to stop the bleeding from a dozen wounds. What brought her to see me originally was a depression so severe that suicide seemed like a reasonable choice. Once she became stabilized, I learned that she was recovering from sexual abuse as a child, from physical abuse at the hands of her current lover, and from frequent bouts of drug and alcohol abuse. When she described herself as "in recovery," I thought to myself, "For now and forever."

In addition to these challenges, which were certainly enough work for any two or three mortals, Martha also suffered from an eating disorder of the binge-vomiting variety. She was anxious, prone to panic attacks, mood swings, and self-destructive acts. She had conflicts at work, was not speaking to most members of her family, and had engaged in a series of promiscuous adventures with the "dregs of the earth." Naturally, she had been in therapy most of her life and had been hospitalized on two occasions for nervous exhaustion and depression and another time for alcohol withdrawal.

Although I cannot explain exactly why, I believed in Martha. I never labelled her with any of a dozen possible diagnoses that would have fit. I ignored the two inches of case notes that were part of her medical history. I overlooked the fact that this was a spectacularly disturbed woman who had always been troubled and, likely, always would be. To me, she seemed wonderfully engaging. Martha was the most interesting person I had ever known—witty, creative, spontaneous, unpredictable, wracked with the anguish of a life in turmoil. I did not romanticize her suffering, but neither did I assume that the shape she was in was as bad as she, and everyone else, assumed. I told her she just lacked direction. She had boundless energy but nowhere to focus her talents, and she was extremely bright and talented. After twenty years' experience as a client in therapy, she knew more than I ever would about the process. She was insightful, articulate, personable, and thoroughly entertaining. Because she liked me as much as I liked her, we worked together for a few years. I believed in her and, just as importantly, she believed in me. We believed in one another. We told each other that a lot.

Martha improved at a pace and scale that even I could not have imagined. She dumped her destructive boyfriends, reestablished contact with her family, confronted her father, and improved her relationships at work. She stopped using alcohol and drugs. She met a stable man she loved, married him, and had a baby. Her bouts of depression became less frequent and less intense. When she did feel down, she no longer resorted to overeating or fantasies of suicide. She quit her job, went to graduate school, and became a therapist herself, and a fine one at that.

I am utterly blown away by the power of believing in someone. I never saw Martha as sick but as eccentric. I never treated her as disabled but as lazy. I talked to her not as a patient but as an equal.

After that experience, I felt like a kid who had been pretending that he had super powers and then one day discovered that the powers were real. Martha helped me to believe in myself.

Holding Hands

It seems that the clients who most moved me were those with whom I enjoyed relatively long-term relationships. Sometimes the details of their lives blend together. A priest struggling with his sexual impulses. A woman dying of cancer. An exhibitionist. A person who hears voices. What did I do for these people? What did they do to move me so?

I held their hands. I got close to them, so close that I knew their every secret, their innermost thoughts, their dreams and fantasies. Nobody had ever been closer to them; perhaps nobody ever would be, though I would like to think that our relationship was just the beginning of intimacy for them, not the end.

Part VIII

. . . .

A Work in Progress

23

Finding a Voice

To this day, I cannot believe that anyone cares to read what I write, much less pays me for the privilege. Writing is something that I have always done for myself because I have no other choice. I write to save myself. I write because it is not work for me; it is among the most pleasurable things that I do.

Given how busy my life is—teaching, consulting, parenting, seeing a few clients—I am often asked how I find the time to write, especially considering the sheer number of books I am often working on at the same time. I am always puzzled by that question: I don't have to *find* the time to write, any more than I have to find the time to work out each morning, to brush my teeth, or to eat a meal. It is what I do.

The follow-up question, then, is, "So, *when* do you find the time to write?" I find that one just as puzzling. My response is, "Why, whenever I can!" I sometimes write for a few hours in the early morning when the rest of the world sleeps. I write between my classes. I will write for several hours on the weekend. I even write sometimes when I am driving (I have taught myself to scribble on a pad without looking).

This may sound like the confession of a workaholic (or writeaholic), and if that term includes the irresistible compulsion to continue this activity, I plead guilty. I suppose my writing would be really out of control if I did it to the point where my other responsibilities and pleasures—my "day job," my family and friends, and my leisure activities—suffered as a result. I don't think this is the case. For me, writing is as much a part of my life as gardening or knitting is to someone else. It helps me relax. It centers me. It is the driving force of my life.

Where Did the Force Come From?

When somebody turns out to be particularly good at something—hitting a curve ball, acting or singing, building or discovering things, or making money—we tend to look at childhood experiences for signs of precociousness. In our search to explain a talent, a success story, or a string of productivity, we want to figure out what it was that programmed the individual to take a different path from others. We do this as much to be able to duplicate this template with our own children as to reassure ourselves that the same fate will not befall us.

When I read about the early years of writers, sure enough, the talent was there to find for anyone who cared to look. Perhaps nobody looked too hard in my case, but I can find no such evidence of early talent. I still have nightmares of sitting in school trying to learn grammar. To this day, I cannot tell the difference between the subject and object of a sentence. I know what verbs are—they are action words—but the rest eludes me and always has. This means that I was not exactly encouraged to pursue the craft of writing. I never learned the intricacies. I did not have a particularly strong vocabulary or a mastery over language. In any case, I certainly did not have much to say that anyone would have been interested in.

I never thought of myself as a writer growing up, nor did I ever aspire to be one. It is as if this force within me was hiding all those years, hibernating, waiting for the right moment to show itself. When I first realized I might have something to say, it surprised me more than anyone else. When my first book was rejected by thirty-six publishers, I was too stubborn to stop. I already had a lifetime of experience in dealing with rejection.

Writing is something that now comes extraordinarily easily for me. I don't agonize over how to say things. I don't feel blocked. The words just flow out of me. This is not to say that writing is not the most difficult thing that I do, because it is. The greatest challenge, however, is not in getting the words out the first time, but in the subsequent revisions that involve dialogues with reviewers and editors. This, of course, is the part of writing that is most crucial, that makes the difference between a bit of self-indulgence and a genuinely moving passage that speaks to others.

How did a mediocre student from inner-city public education, with no mentors or support, develop a talent to write? Even more interesting, how did I ever find my own voice? I don't have any definitive answers to these questions. I can make stuff up, frame it in psychological terms, and sufficiently obscure the subject so as to leave you confused enough that I can move on to something else. I wonder if it is ever possible to explain anything about a complex human life. I know this is what writers and therapists are supposed to do, and I do it fairly well, but I suspect more often than not we are just providing some illusion of truth in a vast inexplicable landscape.

In my case, my voice came to me so slowly I can name no single point at which I felt born as a writer. College is supposed to be a time for experimentation, and its atmosphere did encourage me. I began a journal, which I have kept to this day, to sort out my confusion and pain. Even after twenty-five years, I still cannot read these entries without feeling my chest ache. I was filled with anguish over lost loves and unreachable dreams. I was despondent and depressed, alone and lonely, suicidal at times.

My journal was the one place I could turn to for comfort, the one place I could pour out my heart. There was a purity in that writing, even if I tended toward the melodramatic. I felt good that I could express reasonably clearly what was going on inside me. That was the very beginning of the voice within me, the capacity to describe what I see and hear, and most important, what I think and feel.

A few professors along the way, reading and reacting to my term papers, validated that I had a valuable resource that could be developed, a force that could be captured. I know this sounds simplistic—an authority told me I was good, and I believed him, and so believed in myself. That, however, is substantially what took place. In many ways, I think that believing in others is a basis for everything I have done since then as a teacher and therapist. Of course, one must be speaking the truth. It is not useful to tell someone she is good at something when she is not. But I have always found it easy to find something in another person that is redeemable and that can be nurtured, some talent that is waiting to find its voice.

One professor in graduate school is primarily responsible for awakening in me an image of myself as a writer. He noticed or, at least, labelled my talent. He encouraged me to write and to do so every day, to think of myself as a writer so I could become one. Although he wished to mold me in his own image, and I worked very hard to please him, this relationship became the impetus for me to find *a* voice, even if it was not *my* voice.

We conducted a lengthy correspondence over the years, in both letters and tapes, and this structure provided the foundation for my transition from apprentice to professional. Once I began writing every day to an audience other than myself, even if it was an audience of one, I made the commitment to continue this habit.

Why I Write

Now that I have found my voice, or at least my voice for this time in my life, the remaining question is why I continue to follow this force with such dedication and zeal. It can't be for money, because none of my books has ever made enough even to pay for my time. If I am writing for pure fun and enjoyment of the process, then why do I work on half a dozen books at the same time, plus the same number of articles?

While it's true that writing is one way that I attempt to work through my personal issues, it is also the primary means by which I define myself. That is one reason for my drive to write; however, there are others.

Recognition and Validation

I thrive on others' telling me I am special. While I am no longer addicted to such flattery, it still sure feels good. I hear sports figures, actors and singers, pop icons and celebrities complain about all the attention they receive, and I understand there can be too much of a good thing. Like many people, however, I would like the opportunity to explore the limits of my tolerance.

I care very little for money. There is nothing I don't have that I particularly want. If I had more money I would just buy a bigger house, a more expensive car, give away nicer presents. Nothing much else would change for me. Fame is another story. It feels wonderful to be approached by strangers who want a hug because they feel close to me. I love getting mail from people who want to talk about things I have written. I have yet to tire of the invitations to speak at various points on the planet. I realize this is recognition on a very small scale, but it nevertheless feels wonderful.

Influence

I am a writer and a teacher because of the kick I get out of making a difference to others. What I experience as a therapist in affecting the life of a single individual is magnified ten or twenty times when, as a teacher, I reach hundreds at the same time. When I consider that tens of thousands of people may read these words, or that hundreds of thousands may hear me in the media talking about my books, I feel dizzy.

Wow! What an incredible honor and privilege to reach out to so many people, to touch their lives. This must be the same kick that politicians feel, at least the ones who run for office because they want to make the world better, not because they want to line their bank accounts and feed their egos. And what kind of credibility would I have if I denied that the pursuit of recognition was a great part of my motivation to write or at least publish what I write? If it were not, I would just have gone on doing all my writing in my private journal.

Creativity

I feel most alive when I am in the process of creating something. Some of the best days I have ever lived were those when I was sitting in a chair with a pen in hand. There are few experiences more exhilarating than looking at a passage I have created that I *know* is good. It feels like my whole day, sometimes my whole week, has been redeemed. Anything else I do that week is extra.

There is definitely a creative force within me that has to get out. If I didn't write, I would *have* to do something else to express myself. This is the force behind my writing that is most pure, that exists regardless of whether anyone sees the writing or not. It is a pleasure in the process of producing the work, not in seeing it completed. In fact, when I have finished a book, after a brief feeling of elation there is a more substantial and lingering mood of depression, and my restless energy pushes me onward to the next project.

If I were my own therapist, I would ask myself what I am hiding from that I have to keep creating at such a frantic pace. I would answer, admittedly defensively, that I am racing against time. There is so much I want to do, so much I want to say, and so little time.

Immortality

No doubt about it; I am terrified of death. I don't for a moment believe that after I take my last breath I will be going to another place, whether that is heaven or hell, reincarnation in another form, or pure energy that is conscious of itself. I will be food for worms. Period.

I am envious of those who have convinced themselves there is a better life waiting for them on the other side. If that should happen, won't it be a pleasant surprise! But I'm not holding my breath.

I have discovered, I am pleased to say, that there is a way to live forever, or at least as long as our species survives. As every teacher, therapist, and parent well realizes, as long as a part of us continues to flourish in those we have helped, we will live forever. Actors who have been dead for decades continue to exist on our screens and in our minds. Authors who have been worm food for centuries still live on today in their words as if the authors themselves were immortal.

I believe writing is one way to cheat death, to live forever. As long as a part of me remains in some obscure corner of a library or a secondhand bookstore and there is a possibility that somebody could pick me up and allow me to talk to him or her, then I will remain alive, regardless of what happens to my body.

Self-Therapy

The subjects I choose for books or articles are always connected to some unresolved issue in my life. The acts of reading all the literature on the topic, integrating it, making sense of what I have studied and observed, and developing guiding principles are powerfully therapeutic.

For example, I am ashamed of what I do when I am alone, how different I am from the self I project to others, so I launch a systematic investigation, interviewing thousands of others. As the book takes shape and I learn what others do during their most private moments, I feel more self-accepting and forgiving. How weird could I really be when I hear similar weirdness in the most intimate stories of a thousand others?

I feel overwhelmed by the complexity of what is involved in helping people change. Furthermore, I have to teach other people to do this kind of work, provide them with the knowledge base they need, the skills that are required, and the attitudes and state of mind that are necessary. How can I do this when I am not sure how and why therapy works? I could not explain even to my twelve-year-old son's satisfaction how it is possible that so many different ways of helping people are all equally helpful. When I do workshops, professionals who are a heck of a lot older, wiser, and experienced than I am ask me questions about why things happen a particular way. They have paid good money for this experience and expect an answer. Yet because they too are therapists, they realize, deep down inside, that there are no definitive answers. They will accept something less than The Truth.

Not so clients who come for help, who demand to know how

something as absurd as talking and listening is supposed to cure their ills: "So what you are saying is that you have no pills for me that will make these disturbing thoughts go away. You will not give me some techniques that I can use to fix my delinquent kid. You can't make my husband treat me any better. And there is nothing you can do to help me lose weight until *I* decide to change. And I'm supposed to pay you for this help? First, I want you to answer some questions: What exactly *will* you do? How will that help? How long will this take? What guarantees do you offer that you can help me?"

Of course, if you know any therapists, you probably realize that this client is not likely to get many satisfying answers.

So a couple of books emerged out of this painful search for acceptable answers to some very reasonable questions. Why do apparently discrepant forms of treatment appear to be useful? How is it possible that a therapist can work in the realm of the unconscious or the conscious, the past or the present, or the domain of feelings, thoughts, or behavior and still make a difference? Why are some practitioners confrontive, others supportive and nurturing, still others aloof and neutral, and yet irrespective of their espoused approaches, they all help their clients? These questions keep me up at night. They cause me to stutter when students or clients press for "real" answers to their queries. What started out as an open letter to my clients became a book about the most powerful operative ingredients in all systems of therapy, regardless of the systems' apparent differences.

Such is the healing that takes place for me when I write. I own a problem more easily once I understand exactly what I am dealing with. In order to speak with authenticity and authority, I have to be able to do what I ask of my readers. When I write a book, I rewrite my life.

I begin to notice a consistent pattern in the conflicts of my life. I keep living through the same struggles again and again, no matter what organization I am part of. In each case, I recognize a tendency to blame another person for tormenting me. It occurs to me that this is what most individuals do when they are in disagreement with others: they decide it is the other person who is at fault. I wonder what this is all about? Can this tendency be stopped, and if so, how? I read everything there is on the subject of conflict, devouring the literature in anthropology, sociology, management, social psychology, education, and ethnology, as if my life depended on it. In a way, it does. The quality of my days (and definitely nights) is compromised by the human battles that I have been part of. These disagreements eat up my time, drain my energy, and leave me feeling frustrated, angry, abused, and misunderstood all at the same time. There must be something I can do. Writing a book on the subject allows me to heal my own interpersonal wounds in an effort to help others do the same.

A colleague and I wrestle with the challenges of an interracial friendship and collaboration. Although worldly and educated, we realize we know very little about one another's cultures and backgrounds. At first cautious, overly solicitous, and tentative, we eventually forge a relationship that is quite trusting and mutually satisfying. We wonder why minorities are so rare in the upper echelons of academia and decide that it is because there are so few mentors and protégés who can bridge their cultural differences. We decide to write about our experiences together, hoping that others may profit from what we learned.

I am riddled with doubts about my competence as a healer. I feel terribly guilty about how little I do, how uncertain I am about the potency of my profession. So deep is my confusion that a whole series of books emerges as a result. Like a long-term therapy case that uncovers layer after layer until the core issues are uncovered and dealt with, I continue to struggle onward. Books fly out of me as fast as my hands can type—five volumes on this subject and counting.

I am indeed puzzled by questions about how I find the time to write. This does not feel like a choice that I make. I do it because I have to. The alternative of remaining silent is unthinkable. I would explode.

24

Healing Myself

I am bleeding internally. I can tell because there is a dull ache radiating from within. It doesn't go away when I change positions. Even after a fitful night's sleep, I can still feel the wound seeping, the blood slowly draining.

There is no medical treatment for this type of hemorrhage; it was inflicted by another's actions and words, not by any physical weapon. Nevertheless, the pain is just as real.

I am angry, really angry. This is unusual for me. I also feel hurt and vulnerable. I decide that I don't like feeling this way. I would prefer to spend my time doing something else, *anything* other than sitting around bleeding to death. Okay, then, let it go. Just like that, I decide to do just that. The bleeding slows, then coagulates into a nice scab that I can pick at my leisure. Even though the wound is inside me.

I healed myself for the moment. I did to myself what I do with others. What did I do? I wonder. It happened so fast. One moment there I was walking into the pharmacy to buy some aspirin, the next instant I feel free of the burden that was plaguing me. Oh, I can bring the pain back any time I wish. Just now, I am teasing myself with the possibility, just as a child who has captured a spider underneath a cup periodically peeks to make certain it has not escaped. Yup, it's still there. I checked. Then I put it back out of sight, out of mind.

The Healing Has No End

What good is my being a healer if I can't apply what I know to help myself? What I know is that I am terribly insecure, all too vulnerable to those who wish to attack my credibility. I also make a great target; I am not exactly inconspicuous. As hard as I try to be nice to everyone, to treat others as I like to be treated myself, to ingratiate myself, I still attract my fair share of trouble from others who seem to feel the need to put me in the place they feel I belong. I suppose that I am sometimes threatening, not necessarily by design but as a consequence of being good at what I do. In all fairness, I probably invite trouble as well—I am sometimes thoughtless and insensitive in spite of my resolve to do good whenever I can. There are also times when I seek retribution against those who I believe have done me wrong.

Certainly, I contribute to the ongoing conflicts. I refuse to back down. I am able to muster considerable support among my colleagues, making me a definite threat to the existing power base. Yet I have no threatening aspirations. I just want to be left alone to do my work. I don't want anyone trying to control me, and I don't wish to control anyone else. One antagonist calls me a "loose cannon" because I operate differently than he thinks I should. He wants me to be just like him, and to the extent that I speak my own mind, I must be brought under control.

Sometime, I guess, I will have to accept the fact that no matter how hard I try not everyone is going to like me. Until I can heal myself of this neurotic need (and it does feel like a need rather than a preference), I will continue to be limited in what I do and how I do it. How wonderful it would be to not care what others think! I have known people who *appear* to think that way, but they are not the kind of folks I aspire to be like, and I have always suspected they were lying to themselves and to me.

Being a good therapist, teacher, and writer often involves saying and doing things that are not likeable. I suppose that could be one definition of all three jobs: they involve telling people things that they would rather not hear but need to attend to if they are going to move beyond where they are. I try not to play it safe in any of these three arenas, and the risks that I take in revealing myself involve facing my worst nightmares.

I take similar risks with hiking and climbing. I hate heights, not because I am afraid of falling but because in a single impulsive moment I might jump. Yet I force myself to go on expeditions to places where I am terrified. I cannot look down. I feel light-headed. Over and over in my head, I hear a voice that says, "All you have to do is let go and it would all be over. Don't you wonder what it would be like to fall? All your worries would be over. You could just let go. It's not so hard. . . ." I hate it. I hate it! But I force myself to keep going up to these places, to overcome the fear. I had hoped, with experience, the voice would get tired and go away, but it is my constant companion. The same is true with taking the risk of being myself. I am trying to show myself completely unclothed, free of the posturing that I am aware of and the games I play to get others to like me. I hate putting myself on the line like this, but it's like climbing mountains—I can't stop.

So the healing goes something like this: I don't complain about how frightening the view is on top of the mountain; that is what I went up there for. I look straight ahead and forge onward. So why should I be surprised when I reveal myself to others in an authentic way, stripped of the dressing that makes me more appetizing, and some people find me not all that desirable? Does that not come with the territory? If I really want others to like me so much, why don't I act more compliantly, predictably, and traditionally? The answer is that I want it both ways: I want to be completely honest and then I want to be liked and admired for my honesty. Well, good for me that this is what I want, but what a fool I am to expect that it will happen!

The process of healing myself of the personal doubts, uncertainties, and self-defeating attitudes that are so prevalent throughout this book is an ongoing journey, not unlike the path anyone would take who seeks some sort of relief. What I have going for me, beyond the unique skills of a professional helper, is the determination to forge ahead. I do this knowing that my efforts will never be enough.

Voices of the Past

I have healed myself by being honest about who I am and what I do. I entertain few illusions. A photographer's eye is one that continually frames images of the world in such a way that a few objects stand out more clearly. That is the way I look at the world. Those few clear objects are all that I have ever claimed to offer.

But seeing these objects clearly, even through a single reflex lens, is not enough. There are also voices to listen to. It is true: I hear voices constantly—not the voices of a divine being telling me to go on a pilgrimage or eat oat bran, but the voices of my past. I hear people telling me what they want me to do, how I should be in order to please them. They tell me I should be more like them, more compliant and more cooperative with their agendas. It is hard to breathe when I hear these voices. I hoard them like precious jewels and bring them out when I am complacent, for the effect of hearing these critical judgments is that they only harden my resolve to follow my own voice. I hear the same things over and over inside my head—as I drift off to sleep or more often as I lie perfectly still in bed pretending to sleep, hoping to trick the sandman into leaving a few grains. The most painful messages are ones that I play over and over: "You are selfish." "You are unprofessional." "You are a loose cannon." "You don't really care." "You are too ambitious." "You are insensitive." "You are judgmental." "You are difficult to be around."

When I get a pimple on my face (weren't they supposed to end with adolescence?), I touch it periodically throughout the day to remind myself that it is still there. I stare at it in the mirror, note its placement, try to predict its growth pattern. I turn over a little part of my brain to this pimple, to monitor it during every moment of its existence no matter what else I am doing. It is the same with these voices. I think of them as blemishes that are growing inside me. Yet these voices help me heal myself. Whether their messages are accurate or not, they force me to reflect continuously on whether they *might* be true. I find that reflection healing. Certainly painful, but also quite helpful. When I attempt to live with the worst that anyone has ever said to me in a moment of anger, I feel stronger. I will keep climbing to the top of the mountain until I can live with fear of heights, even if I can't eliminate it.

Among the voices from the past I also hear messages from all the mentors who have been my models. I hear their words of reassurance, but just as important, I hear the ways they used to work. I have followed their styles, borrowed their best ideas, and adapted their methods in such a way that they work for me.

There is one other set of messages that I hear. It contains the essence of what I say to others: "Where do you want to go and how is this going to get you there?" "What are you doing to create this situation?" "How are you distorting what happened?" One of the best things about being a therapist is that I can test out these messages on others to see how they work. By the time I use them with myself, they have already accumulated an impressive record of success. If they then provide me with some comfort, they are even more powerful in subsequent applications with clients because of my confidence in their utility.

I draw strength from all these voices. I have sorted and organized them in such a way that I can draw on their peculiar gifts as I need them. And it has occurred to me, only as these words are being written, that I have finally stopped imitating the voices of others. The ultimate point so far in my self-healing is that I have finally found the voice that is mine.

25

Therapist as Travel Agent

Being a therapist is very much like working as a travel agent. I sit in my office all day long as people file in and out. They each have a story to tell or, more likely, another installment in a continuing saga that has no discernable beginning and no end in sight. Their lives feel empty, spiritless. They are sick of their routines, bored with those who populate their worlds. They hunger for adventure. They are searching for something different, something more than they already have. And they come to me for guidance.

My job is to listen carefully to what is missing in their lives, then help them crystalize what it is they really want. This is no easy task considering that, in many cases, they don't know what choices are available or they are afraid to dream. I help them to articulate where they have always wanted to go—back to school, to another job or a new location, into a new relationship, on a trip in time and space, or on a journey in attitude. Once they have identified the destination, it is my job to help them get there. Just as a travel agent displays an assortment of brochures, I describe the allures of emotional paradise: "Just imagine yourself free of those feelings that drag you downward." I help make the arrangements for the journey, book the accommodations along the way, and remain available throughout the trip in case there are any unforeseen delays or emergencies. Finally, I hear the stories upon the client's return. Then, frankly, I am jealous as hell.

Here I am still sitting in my office, doing essentially the same things the same way, while listening to reports of exciting adventures. I hear about new territories that have been explored and exotic locales that have been visited. I see convincing evidence that these travelers are indeed quite different—more vibrant and worldly. I ask myself, What have I done lately?

I have got to travel. It is in my blood. I can't sit still. I want to see everything, meet everyone. I don't want to listen to other people's adventures; I want to create my own. There is nothing worse than a travel agent who has never traveled anywhere, whose sole sources of knowledge about the world are vicarious—the stories of others' experience.

Keep Moving

I have mentioned that one reason the darkness I fear does not engulf me is the fervor with which I keep moving. I am dedicated to the pursuit of adventure in all its variant forms. I want to see everything on this planet and make the acquaintance of every person worth knowing. While I realize the lunacy of this mission, I don't feel sufficiently discouraged to give it up altogether. After all, the ultimate goal is a whole lot less important than the process.

It is not just where I go that is important, or even how long I stay, but rather how I travel. I will not board tour buses or stand in line for anything; I rarely enter museums. I will not be recognized or identify myself as a tourist. Even if I should stand out, as I am likely to by my appearance, accent, and manner, I do not travel for pure entertainment but to exchange ideas. I want to be turned upside-down, to be challenged to reassess what is most important.

When a witch doctor tells me that unless I am careful I will become infected by the pain of my clients, the whole way that I view therapy is forever altered.

When a cab driver in Kuala Lumpur tells me he works twelve hours per day, seven days a week, and has done so most of his adult life, I rethink what it means to say, "I don't own my life."

When a Swedish woman tells me she is not interested in knowing me or even talking to me, only in having a brief sexual interlude, I am flattered only as long as it takes to realize that I now know what women mean when they say they feel like a piece of meat in the eyes of leering men.

When a woman in Fiji smiles at me with the unrestrained openness of someone who has love in her heart for everyone she meets, I resolve to follow her lead. I commit myself to smile more myself, to be nice to strangers I meet.

When a reporter in Lima becomes indignant after I question her about why she is an hour late for our appointment, I am taught a new conception of time, one that is elastic enough to accommodate unforeseen encounters that may occur on your way to wherever you think you are going.

When I observe myself arguing with a Haitian woman over the cost of a mahogany figurine, feeling so satisfied with the few dollars I am saving, I realize that what was spare change to me was a week's wages for her. I feel pitiful.

When I stand alone on a beach or a glacier in New Zealand, surrounded as far as I can see by rugged, solitary scenery, I wonder why I get so worked up over things back home that don't matter. I return, only to meet a fellow teacher who admonishes me to make every future decision based on one and only one principle: How will what I am about to do or what my colleagues and I are discussing benefit students? I have used that as my measure of critical significance ever since.

When I sit at the bottom of the Grand Canyon, my back to a rock wall reaching up to the sky, watching the muddy water swirl by, I think how much work it took to get to this place. My back and feet ache. There are hours left to go before I will rejoin the comforts of camp and companionship. Yet I know that the degree of appreciation I have for this special setting is directly proportionate to the amount of effort it took me to get here.

Travel, for me, is about hardship as well as indulgent pleasures. It means being herded with crowds before I can break free. It inevitably involves delays, lost sleep, and being lost. If it is not merely a vacation, if the travel is undertaken to enlighten as well as relax, then the best part is taking what I have learned home. If I am going to spend hundreds or thousands of dollars visiting somewhere, I want a heck of a lot more than a few photographs and souvenirs to show for the experience. I expect and demand to be somehow different afterwards. I am, therefore, never surprised when I am made different.

It's Not the Place, It's the People

The sound of the sea calls me as loudly as a morning bugler. I carefully lace up my dirty white running shoes and head out across the Peruvian desert, up over dunes, and across dried seaweed beds bordering the land of flamingos to a museum that supposedly houses relics dug from the earth. It is a four-mile trek, each way, the way of the condor.

My already sunburned face starts to smart from the reflections off the rippled ground and the sweat running down. I have a good stride going, slow breathing through my nose, mind centered on where to place my next step, my run paralleling the shore. At first, I hear nothing. Then the birds start to trumpet my entry onto their sacred ground. They cautiously edge away on their gawky legs, pretending indifference, but watching my movements closely. A pelican with an immense wing span skims the water's surface, hunting, occasionally flapping its great wings for balance. Smaller birds sit quietly, eating their Sunday brunch.

I ask them directions. I am assuredly lost. I decide to follow car tracks—from nowhere, leading nowhere. I feel thirst, but not yet fatigue. I bound over several dunes and in the distance I see a building. Another mile and I can see that I have reached my destination—the museum.

All the doors are shut tight even though a sign displays the hours: "Sundays, 8–6." It is 9:04 A.M. I peek through an open window in the door of what appears to be the courtyard to the caretaker's home. I can hear children playing. There is a man standing in the yard washing clothes but looking confused. I yell to him, "Señor!" He freezes. Even his smile stays congealed. I yell again and again but he remains persistently immobile. After five minutes, I decide to admire his patience. But he seems to have far more than I, this man, lost in his own simple world that sports an idiotic grin. I shrug. Just another one of those unexplained phenomena in a foreign land.

I turn and begin the long run back, not terribly disappointed. I don't much like museums; I like people.

I never know what to make of those who claim New Orleans is a great city, or Australia is a great country, or that any particular place that was created by people, for people, is somehow special, better than other places. Certainly both the bayou and the land down under can be delightful places to visit, but much depends on whom you meet along the way.

I once spent two days trying to hitchhike out of Austria, an experience that led me to vow I would never return. I have no idea what that country is like, but the few people I met there were not especially nice to me. Peru, on the other hand, was a place of magic. Here was a country falling apart at the seams. Terrorists kept knocking out the electricity in the city, forcing me to lecture in the dark. Thievery was out of control to the point that inhabitants took their windshield wipers with them when they left their cars. Inflation was so high my salary was paid in a suitcase of near worthless money. For six months, I never saw the sun in Lima, a city covered in mist throughout winter. We lived without hot water and slept in a bed full of fleas. So why do I love that country so? It has nothing to do with the mountains, the sea, the cities, the ruins, museums, restaurants, and sights. It was the people I met who charmed me, including the frozen man standing in the courtyard of the desert museum.

I took the time to learn their language, to study their customs, to understand their culture. This has always been my primary task before I leave home. This preparation also allows me to lose myself along the way.

Living Different Lives

What I like most about traveling, especially when I am on a solo adventure, is that I can be anyone I want and nobody knows it isn't me. Freed from the normal restraints of the structures of my life, the expectations and demands of others, I can be quiet or silly with those I meet, and they assume this is what I am really like.

I can introduce myself as a writer, a teacher, a researcher, a consultant, or a therapist, each label a part of who I am. Each evokes different reactions. Likewise, I may choose to present myself as shy and reflective, assertive and arrogant, or conciliatory to the point of being ingratiating. Once I am wandering in a foreign land, I feel giddy with the thrill of reinventing myself. Since nobody knows the way I am supposed to be, the way I normally act, I can be and do most anything, and it is taken in stride, as if this is who I am.

Travel helps me put distance between who I am and what I do. I define myself according to the roles I play—as my father's son, my son's father, my wife's husband, my clients' therapist, my students' professor, my readers' author. I am defined by others, whether I like it or not—by my gender, my age, my religion, even the neighborhood I live in. When I am on the road, however, these referents become obscured for the reason that I forget who I am.

Travel has taught me to let go of my ambitions and goals, to look around me with both eyes open. I remind myself, again and again, that the ride is more important than the destination.

26

. . . .

Taking Care of Myself

I f I can't take care of myself, I am in no position to do so for others. My work is so draining and challenging that unless I am able to keep myself functioning at optimal levels, both personally and professionally, I am not doing anyone else much good. My growth as a therapist, therefore, has really been about how I have developed as a person.

The most attractive benefit of my profession has always been that the more capable I become of getting what I want in life the better equipped I am to help others do the same. Techniques and therapeutic wizardry are never enough. Neither is the best of intentions. What make a difference in other people's lives are the same things that work quite well in my own.

It is when I know, beyond a shadow of a doubt, that certain interventions and strategies will be successful that I can "sell" them most effectively to clients. How can I know for sure? It certainly helps to have practiced these methods before with others and noted their positive outcomes. Even more convincing, however, is when I can be a living example of what the client and I are about to try. I love to be able to say to a client, with passion and unbridled enthusiasm, "Yes, I know exactly what you are going through. I have seen this in others and experienced it myself. There is indeed a way out for you, one that is within reach, but you have to be willing to do some things that will challenging for you."

There are several strategies and interventions that I use routinely to take care of myself and that I suggest wholeheartedly to others.

Exercising

Almost everyone thinks that exercising is a good idea. It helps people who are anxious to calm down. It loosens the tenacious grip of depression. It is probably the single best all-around therapeutic activity that anyone could begin and stick with if the intention is to increase self-esteem and general well-being.

I can be quite convincing in lauding the benefits of an exercise program, not only because I am familiar with the research on the subject but also because I have seen what it has done for me. I started running twenty years ago, the day my mother died of heart failure and my father lay in the hospital having a coronary bypass operation, both of them about the same age I am now. Although I began the regimen originally as a way to prolong my life, most of the benefits have been psychological rather than physical. I use exercise as self-medication for stress and as a way to burn off excess energy that keeps me awake at night. I have grown as a therapist because I feel so good about myself, beginning my days as I do with an activity that is so self-nurturing.

Make no mistake; there is little about working out that is fun. It is painful, uncomfortable, time-consuming, and annoying. I exercise every day. No exceptions. No excuses. It is not an option for me any more than is brushing my teeth. If I don't run or bike or work out, I don't sleep well at night. During the day, I feel negligent.

I feel particularly good about having been able to sustain this part of my commitment to take care of my body for so long and in spite of excuses I could easily create. My pain threshold has increased and, therefore, my tolerance for other forms of discomfort. My body image is ideal: I like the way I look. I don't get sick. I feel light on my feet and comfortable inside my body.

Eating

The other part of my commitment to take care of my body involves what I put into my mouth. Since I grew up in a home in which both parents were addicted to cigarettes and my mother abused both food and alcohol, I saw firsthand the effects of being out of control. On the same day I decided to take care of my heart for the rest of my life, I also changed the way that I ate.

I am very careful what I put into my body. I deprive myself of the things that I once enjoyed the most—hamburgers, Häagan Dazs ice cream, spareribs, salami, omelettes. Yet I don't feel any particular deprivation, nor do I feel tempted to sample these treats any longer. I now associate them with my own demise and have learned to appreciate other foods that don't wreak havoc in my arteries. Of course, it always helps to be able to conjure up the image of my mother, now long dead, and my father, who has been crippled by a stroke in spite of his preventive surgery. It feels healing for me to take care of my body, to keep myself trim and fit.

Self-Talk

This is the best part of being a therapist and growing to be a better one. All day long, we healers tell people stuff that is intended to change the ways they think about themselves and their predicaments. Reframing, when we suggest alternative views of a situation, can be almost magical in its power.

I practiced reframing for myself today (as I do every day), when I was feeling overwrought by my dilemma over whether I should stay in my present position (in which I am perfectly content) or give in to the temptations of another institution that is offering me the sun and the moon to jump ship. At first, I felt the weight of a tremendous burden, that is until I reframed the two sides of the dilemma as two lovely possibilities, each of which provides me with great opportunities. I could hardly make a mistake in this decision if I tried.

Therapists spend a lot of time confronting the silly, dysfunctional ways that people think about their life situations. Clients trap themselves by their language and by their beliefs that keep them powerless. I was doing just that when I was saying to myself, "What a pain that I have to face this decision when everything was going so smoothly. No matter what I do, I am going to feel regretful that I missed out on something." Or, "This is bad news that I have to face this right now—I either traumatize my kid with another move during a vulnerable time in his life, or I give up my one chance to move up to the big leagues as a major player."

Of course, such internal thinking is nonsense, a gross distortion of reality. I confront people all the time who have similar exaggerated conceptions of their plight. Once again, I find that the best part of this job is that as I help to heal others, I also heal myself. It is because I have heard myself all these years talking other people out of their internal traps that I can do so quite capably with myself. I talk to myself. Constantly. I repeat the therapeutic messages that I dish out to others. If they don't work with me, I don't bother using them with others. At least several times each day, like meditative chants, I hear echoing in my brain a continual stream of the messages I described earlier:

"Remember what is *really* important."

"What can I tell myself differently about this, to change how I am feeling?"

"How can I be more loving?"

"How am I exaggerating or distorting what is happening?"

"A hundred years from now, none of this will matter."

"Go for it!"

"I can do this. I really can do this."

The list goes on and on, each whisper a reminder that I have the power to take care of myself.

Keeping a Journal

When I was seventeen years old, I began a journal to record all the frightening, exciting changes that were going on inside my body and mind. I have kept it going ever since, the pages now overfilling a file cabinet. This repository has been one of the primary means by which I have grown as a therapist and a human being; it has been my therapist and lifelong companion.

I can look back at any time in my life and tell you what I was doing, what I was struggling with, which issues I was coming to terms with. I can recognize the central themes of my life as they are playing themselves out this moment because I am a student of my own past.

I think of my journal writing in the same terms that I do my running: most of the time, I would rather do something else. However, I learned long ago that anything that is worth doing takes a lot of work, the kind of commitment that lasts a lifetime, not just an inspired moment. I think that most clients understand this as well, even though their original intention is for a quick fix in which I do most of the work.

When I say to clients that in order to make the improvements they would like, they are going to have to do no less than change the ways they relate to the world, themselves, and everyone else, I see a look of panic on their faces, as if they have been given a death sentence. Soon after, however, comes an imperceptible nod, an acknowledgment that this is the truth they have known all along.

Most everyone thinks that, just like exercising or healthy eating, writing in a journal is a good idea. It helps us to set goals for the future as well as make sense of the past. It is a safe place to talk to ourselves, to work through problems, to articulate clearly what we are thinking, doing, and feeling. Writing in a journal is one way that I have taken care of myself, confronting on a weekly, sometimes daily, basis what I am doing and where I am headed. I can do that for myself just as I do that with others.

Loving

Relationships are everything. I became a therapist in the first place partly because of my hunger for intimacy. One of the most enjoyable aspects of my work has been the opportunity to be close to so many people who have trusted me. I have felt throughout much of my life that I what I do primarily is love people for a living.

I have felt redeemed by the privilege to help others, but that has hardly been enough. Relationships in my own life have been the source of my capacity to be loving in my work. It has been a struggle for me to allow others to take care of me, a circumstance that I have associated with vulnerability. To this day, I am uncomfortable asking people to do things for me but delighted to offer myself to them. It feels like a luxury to ask my son to retrieve something for me, to ask my wife if she would mind doing me a favor, to ask a friend for a ride to the airport. I have a graduate assistant and secretary at work, yet I feel apologetic whenever I ask them to do something, even though it is part of their jobs.

I have learned to be more loving by allowing my friends and family to take care of me. It is impossible for any single individual, no matter how independent, resourceful, or capable, to take care of himself or herself without the support of others. I have been fortunate in that regard. I have had a stable, loving wife and son who have compensated for the jolts I suffered during childhood, a couple of inspiring mentors who extended themselves to me during critical times in my development, a few excellent therapists who helped free me of my most self-destructive urges, and the support of friends who have helped me feel that I really do belong on this planet, that I am not the alien that I have felt myself to be.

Never Enough

One principal theme that runs throughout this book is that no matter what I do and how much I accomplish, it is never enough. I am always on probation, only as worthy as my latest success. I may justify compulsive achieving as striving for excellence, but I also recognize that I am grasping for something that is out of reach. Never satisfied with where I am, I am always planning the next step. I am constantly in motion, moving onward, mind racing with ideas that I will never have the time to put into action. I cannot sit still.

Each night before I fall asleep, I want to be able to say to myself that I lived that day to its fullest, that I did not waste a moment. If I am not doing something worthwhile or not engaged in some form of active leisure, I feel guilty. Yet, somehow, among all of the productive things that I find time to complete, I also read fiction, go hiking in the mountains, watch my son's baseball games, launch him into the world every morning, go out to lunch with friends, and lead a very active social life, as well as a quite satisfying marriage. Needless to say, I hate to sleep.

One would think I was a perfect candidate for stress disorders or a heart attack. Yet my resting heart rate is fifty, my usual manner is quite low key, and most of the time I feel rested and relaxed. I am virtually always in a good mood. I love what I am doing and can't wait to wake up tomorrow and start again. I am a workaholic *and* a playaholic.

I am also haunted by missed opportunities. It is hard for me to say no to any invitation to do something; I am afraid it is my last chance. I am most regretful about all the time I spent in the early part of my life not doing some things that I really wanted to. Most of my adolescence was spent at the local shopping mall, ostensibly to meet girls whom I never had the courage to approach much less ask out.

To this day, I lament all the time I spent trolling malls for an imagined love. When I think about all the places I could have visited, all the new experiences I could have had, all the people I could have met, I kick myself in exasperation. Any pain that a girl could have inflicted on me by declining my invitation was nothing compared to what I have done to myself since. I can live quite easily with making a decision to take a risk and not having it work out; what I can't abide is passing up a risk that could have worked out wonderfully.

Why My Life Works

The paradox of this book and of my life is that I can be so flawed and yet so effective. As imperfect as I may be, I still find ways to carry on at quite high levels, both at work and at play. I am a living example of what an ordinary person can do with extraordinary dedication and perseverance.

My life works because:

I can do what I ask of others. Whether it involves trusting, confronting, or setting and reaching goals, I have practiced in my life what I teach to others. I have the fervor of the true believer because whatever I present in the way of strategies for counteracting dysfunctional behaviors has worked with me first.

I am a fearless risk-taker. I am not content to settle for mediocrity, at least in the domains that are within my control. In my relationships, in my work, in the way I conduct my life, I am willing to risk losing what I have (with no regrets) in order to obtain something more fulfilling.

I am working toward accepting my imperfections. Every human being is as complex and paradoxical as I am. We must honor that complexity. I accept my limitations, at least the ones that I don't seem to be able to do much about (those involving my innate talents) and that seem to have desirable side effects (my productivity).

However, I have given up trying to reconcile the discrepancies that make up who I am with who I am supposed to be. We therapists are supposed to be impervious, detached, removed from our clients and their predicaments.

That is a great lie.

I am affected *profoundly* by anyone I have ever tried to help.

I am bleeding internally.

The price I pay for caring so much is that I live under the specter of falling short of my expectations. This is not something I intend to change. What I have learned, however, from opening myself up to the self-scrutiny in these pages is that I will never be enough, and that *is* good enough.

About the Author

Jeffrey A. Kottler is professor of counseling and educational psychology at the University of Nevada, Las Vegas. He travels throughout the world lecturing on the subjects discussed in his seventeen books. Most recently, he is the author of *On Being a Therapist* and *Beyond Blame: A New Way of Resolving Conflicts in Relationships*.